WHAT WOULD THEY SAY?

The Founding Fathers

on

Current Issues

Edited with supplement by
GLEN GORTON

HUNTINGTON HOUSE PUBLISHERS

Huntington House Publishers
P.O. Box 53788
Lafayette, Louisiana 70505

Library of Congress Card Catalog Number 97-77564
ISBN 1-56384-146-0

Cover: Patrick Henry Before the Virginia House of
Burgesses (1851) by Peter F. Rothermel.
Red Hill, The Patrick Henry National Memorial,
Brookneal, Virginia

Contents

PART THREE
-Documents-

Foreword

Never before in human history have so many brilliant minds assembled in one place as in the hot Summer of 1787 in Philadelphia. Here this collection of America's greatest patriots—John Adams, Benjamin Franklin, George Mason, George Washington, John Jay, and, of course, James Madison—came together to write the United States Constitution.

The famous American historian James M. Beck wrote many years ago: "The framers of the Constitution were great clock-makers in the science of statecraft, and they did, with admirable ingenuity, put together an intricate machine, which promised to run indefinitely, and tell the time of the centuries." And it has told the time of centuries. The U.S. Constitution is not just the most revered political document in American history—it is the most revered political document in world history.

How depressing that the modern day politicians now ignore the advice and warnings of our founding fathers. Living in Washington and meeting with congressmen on an almost daily basis, I sometimes wonder whether even a single one of the 535 today—who routinely ignore and in some cases wantonly trample the constitution—have even a fraction of the wisdom of the group that came together to give birth to this great nation 200 years ago.

The modern-day subversion of the Constitution is reflected in the dramatic growth of government in recent decades. In the early years of the republic, government was limited and lean. It bore scarcely no resemblance to the colossal empire it has evolved into today. In 1800 the federal government employed 3,000 people and had a budget of less than ($100 million in today's dollars). That's a far cry from today's $1,700,000 million federal budget and the government's 3 million person workforce.

From its frugal beginnings, the United States federal government now subsidizes every conceivable private activity from Belgian endive research to maple syrup production to the advertising of the Pillsbury dough boy in Europe and Japan. In a recent moment of high drama during oral presentations of a case before the supreme Court involving the application of the Interstate Commerce Clause, a bewildered Justice Scalia pressed the Clinton Administration Solicitor General to name even a single activity or program that our modern-day Congress might undertake that would fall outside of the bounds of the Constitution. The stunned Clinton appointee could not think of one. James Madison must have been rolling over in his grave!

The behemoth federal enterprise that we have today in Washington is not the kind of government—limited in federal power—that our forefathers envisioned.

I was recently sadly struck by a news story in the morning papers. A majority of American high school students in a recent poll thought that the Marxist credo "From each according to their ability, to each according to their need," was language from the U.S. Constitution.

All of this is to say that we are in a state of constitutional crisis in America Today. There can be little doubt. Ignorance of the Constitution is widespread. Meanwhile, the Courts and the Congress that are sworn to uphold the letter of the Constitution, feel compelled to rewrite it—to fail to protect the liberties that are guaranteed and to create new "rights"—racial preferences and welfare, for example—out of thin air. Ironically, the death wound that has been driven into the constitution has been placed there by precisely those who insist that they want to make it "a living document."

To argue that we return to the spirit and the true meaning of this "living document" and to listen to the wit and wisdom of the Founding Fathers is to invite a look of scorn, malice, or outright disbelief from modern-day intellectuals. One is accused of trying to "turn back the clock" when urging that government be guided by the original intent of the constitution. And so few make the case. This ultimately has left government free to invade one area of our life and economic liberties after another. So not surprisingly, our liberties seem to be falling like a row of dominoes.

I read through Glen Gorton's book What Would They Say?—the quotations and the biographies—with a sense of overwhelming pride and admiration for the ingeniousness of the architects of our Constitution. This is a book of precious historical treasures. It now rests prominently in my book case—next to my copy of the United States Constitution.

—STEPHEN MOORE
DIRECTOR OF FISCAL POLICY STUDIES
AT THE CATO INSTITUTE

In remembrance of
Joseph Warren
and our other heroes who fell
for our freedom.

For all
who love that freedom.

Introduction

"No longer virtuous, no longer free," warned Benjamin Franklin over two hundred years ago. If this is merely ancient sophistry, the contents of this book, though perhaps intriguing, will be to a large degree irrelevant for today's reader. But if true, then the voices of our forefathers contained herein cannot be defined as simple opinion, nor even as objective exhortation, but as a unified, cumulative cry—a cry that the freedom won by virtuous toil, virtuous blood, and virtuous death, will pass away, unmourned, in the moral void of a more progressive and tolerant age.

WHAT WOULD THEY SAY? is a reflection on current social and political issues made by the champions of our most glorious age. Although chiefly a study on government and human nature, a colorful and entertaining array of topics appear throughout its otherwise serious message. In a day when moral relativity (formerly known as licentiousness) is hailed by many as the great freedom for which our fathers fought, this book celebrates the ageless proposition that human greatness lies, above all else, in moral excellence. In example a single name is offered: George Washington, who once declared: *"I hope I shall always possess firmness and virtue enough to maintain what I consider the most enviable of all titles, the character of an honest man."* In truth, it was Washington and our other heroes who fervently labored to bequeath their own shackles, the sweet chains of conscience, to future generations of Americans.

In this brief volume, our founders are not interpreted, nor are their opinions subjected to any creative exposition. With the exception of a brief introduction at the beginning of each chapter, the men themselves are given the floor to speak as they please concerning contemporary matters. For this reason, nothing new will be found in these pages—only the time-tested principles of old. Each generation must, in its time, retread these proven paths. These days seem to be our time.

The writings left by these revolutionaries are so voluminous that a work of this modest size can serve only as a sampler. Its purpose, nonetheless, will have been achieved if it helps to awaken that latent jealousy for liberty, decency, and honor, which must reside, even still, in the hearts of countless Americans. It is to this end that Thomas Jefferson writes:

> . . . *certain forms of government are better calculated than others to protect individuals in the free exercise of their natural rights, and are at the same time themselves better guarded against degeneracy, yet experience has shown, that even under the best forms, those entrusted with power have, in time, and by slow operations, perverted it into tyranny; and it is believed that the most effectual means of preventing this would be to illuminate as far as practicable the minds of the people at large, and more especially to give them knowledge of those facts, which history exhibits, that, possessed thereby of the experience of other ages and countries, they may be enabled to know (selfish) ambition under all its shapes, and prompt to exert their natural powers to defeat its purposes.*

This reference handbook is divided into three primary sections. Part One, the main body of quotations, is categorized into relevant issues of the day as follows: Character; Patriotism; Federal Power; Crime; Taxes; Education; Gun Control; Welfare; Term Limits; Religion. It is not necessary to read in sequence. It would, in fact, be most beneficial to read in order of interest, seeing that curiosity is mother to knowledge. The reader will no doubt find several quotes equally suited to another chapter. Character (1) and Religion (10), for example, are so closely related that the line between them is never quite fixed. In fact, it will become obvious as pages turn that every chapter, in some way or another, points back to chapter 1. While this was not intended, it has proven, by the very nature of things, to be unavoidable.

Part Two consists of a biographical sketch of each of the patriarchs quoted to provide an animated and personal glimpse (largely by their peers) of the men behind the message. Some may prefer to read this section first. Among the 28 contributors were 10 signers of the Declaration of Independence; 6 signers of the Constitution; 7 governors; 4 presidents of the United States; 3 presidents of Congress; 3 generals; 2 chief justices of the Supreme Court, as well as several senators and congressmen.

Part Three serves as an appendix containing the essential documents of our American heritage. These include The Declaration of Independence, The Constitution, and The Bill of Rights.

Something must be said here about language. Except where meaning would be altered, the original wording (with its occasional archaic spelling) has been left untouched. Excessive editing or a paraphrase would strip these stirring addresses of their pristine brilliance, reducing them to mere statements. The old language is solid. More is said with fewer words. Granted, its demands on the intellect are greater, but so are its rewards.

The temptation was strong to include distinguished patriots outside the realm of the founding era. Notwithstanding the excellent writings of such Worthies as Daniel Webster, Abraham Lincoln, and others, the original intent to go back to our roots has been retained. No man was allowed to speak (excepting introductions) but had touched and affected firsthand the birth of the nation. In keeping, therefore, with the purposes of the book, these others were regrettably omitted.

There is a certain aura we feel when we utter the words, *"The Founding Fathers."* To be sure, our parents bore the blemishes of a fallible race, yet even so, our admiration of them is not to be ignored as an irrational romanticism. It is real. It is real because virtue is real. It is real because they are our fathers and they have something to say to their sons. Noah Webster spoke well when he said:

> *It is not our duty as freemen to receive the opinions of any men, however great and respectable, without an examination. But when we reflect that some of the greatest men in America, with the venerable FRANKLIN and the illustrious WASH-INGTON at their head; some of them the fathers and saviors of their country, men who have labored at the helm during a long and violent tempest, and guided us to the haven of peace— and all of them distinguished for their abilities, their acquaintance with ancient and modern governments, as well as with the temper, the passions, the interests and the wishes of the Americans;—when we reflect on these circumstances it is impossible to resist impressions of respect, and we are almost impelled to suspect our own judgements . . . Great confidence therefore should be reposed in the abilities, the zeal and integrity of that respectable body.*

The list of that body shines: Washington, Adams, Hancock, Jefferson, Madison, Franklin, to name but a few. The following pages will be occupied with a single goal: To answer the question, *What would THEY say?* What if these men could walk the halls of congress today? And what if, after 200 years, they could speak, one last time, to the present generation of Americans? Perhaps this is best answered with another question: What DID they say? This, after all, is an inquiry that requires zero speculation. After a few trips to the local library, an average, not-so-politically-minded individual may begin to compile a concrete and irrefutable reply. This book is the result of just such an effort. May there be greater and more extensive endeavors, not by the "experts," but by anyone who is weary of the mealy mush in the public diet and wishes to sink his teeth into something substantial, something solid, and something real.

PART ONE

-Issues-

1

Character

"... appealing to the Supreme Judge
of the world
for the rectitude of our intentions ..."

—The Declaration of Independence

The reader may notice the excessive length of this chapter in relation to the others. This is merely because the founding fathers wrote so excessively on THIS subject. Could there be a reason? After visiting our shores, French philosopher Alexis de Tocqueville observed, "America is great because America is good, and if America ever ceases to be good, America will cease to be great."

There is a difference between liberty and licentiousness. Where inward restraint is present, outward force is superfluous. But when a man's conscience is cast away as an intolerant and inexorable foe, freedom must be subdued by the external regime. As Edmund Burke, the renowned English statesman, noted, "Among a people generally corrupt liberty cannot last long."

It is the bondage of virtue that frees us and freedom that makes us great. This has been the unique American experience as no other nation has known it. In words familiar to us all, it has been the right to life, liberty, and the pursuit of happiness.

Can it be that Providence has not connected the permanent felicity of a nation with its virtue?

George Washington
Farewell Address 1796

The Creator would indeed have been a bungling artist had he intended man for a social animal without planting in him social dispositions . . . I sincerely believe, then, with you in the general existence of a moral instinct. I think it the brightest gem with which the human character is studded, and the lack of it as more degrading than the most hideous of the bodily deformities.

Thomas Jefferson to Thomas Law
1814

I agree perfectly with you that "the moral sense is as much a part of our condition as that of feeling."

John Adams to Thomas Jefferson
1816

There is not in human nature a more wonderful phenomenon; nor in the whole theory of it, a more intricate speculation; than the shiftings, turnings, windings and evasions of a guilty conscience. Such is our unalterable moral constitution, that an internal inclination to do wrong is criminal; and a wicked thought stains the mind with guilt, and makes it tingle with pain.

John Adams
1775

Pursue the interests of your country, the interest of your friends, and your own interest also, with the purest integrity, the most chaste honour. The defect of these virtues can never be made up by all the other acquirements of body and mind. Make these, then, your first object. Give up money, give up fame, give up science, give the earth itself and all it contains, rather than do an immoral act. And never suppose that in any possible situation or under any circumstances it is best for you to do a dishonourable thing, however slightly so it may appear to you. Whenever you are to do a thing, though it can never be known but to yourself, ask yourself how you would act were all the world looking at you, and act accordingly. Encourage all your virtuous dispositions, and exercise them whenever an opportunity arises; being assured that they will gain strength by exercise, as a limb of the body does, and that exercise will make them habitual. From the practice of the purest virtue, you may be assured you will derive the most sublime comforts in every moment of life . . . If you ever find yourself environed with difficulties and perplexing circumstances, out of which you are at a loss how to extricate yourself, do what is right, and be assured that that will extricate you the best out of the worst situations. Though you cannot see, when you take one step, what will be the next, yet follow truth, justice, and plain dealing, and never fear their leading you out of the labyrinth in the easiest possible manner. The knot which you thought a Gordian one, will untie itself before you. Nothing is so mistaken as the supposition that a person is to extricate himself from a difficulty by intrigue, by chicanery, by dissimulation, by trimming, by an untruth, by an injustice. This increases the difficulties tenfold, and those who pursue these methods get themselves so involved at length that they can turn no way but their infamy becomes more exposed. It is of great importance to set a resolution, not to be shaken, never to tell an untruth. There is no vice so mean, so contemptible; and he who permits himself to tell a lie once, finds it much easier to do it a second and third time, till at length it becomes habitual; he tells lies without thinking about it, and truths without the world believing him.

Thomas Jefferson to Peter Carr
1785

Nothing can contribute to true happiness that is inconsistent with duty; nor can a course of action conformable to it, be finally without an ample reward. For, God governs; and he is good.

Benjamin Franklin to Mary Stevenson
1768

To pursue virtue where there is no opposition is the merit of a common man, but to practice it in spite of all opposition is the character of a truly great and noble soul. My friend, let the practice of virtue be your aim; for on that depends your future importance and usefulness in life. Virtuous manners I call such acquired habits of thought and correspondent actions as lead to a steady prosecution of the general welfare of society: Virtuous principles I call such as tend to confirm these habits by superinducing the idea of duty. Virtuous manners are a permanent foundation for civil liberty, because they lead the passions and desires to coincide with the appointments of public law.

Nathaniel Greene to Samuel Ward, Jr.
1771

I think I knew General Washington intimately and thoroughly; and were I called on to delineate his character, it should be in terms like these: His mind was great and powerful, without being of the very first order; his penetration strong, though not so acute as that of a Newton, Bacon, or Locke; and as far as he saw, no judgment was ever sounder. It was slow in operation, being little aided by invention or imagination, but sure in conclusion. Hence the common remark of his officers, of the advantage he derived from councils of war, where hearing all suggestions, he selected whatever was best; and certainly no General ever planned his battles more judiciously. But if disturbed during the course of the action, if any member of his plan was dislocated by sudden circumstances, he was slow in readjustment. The consequence was, that he often failed in the field, and rarely against an enemy in station, as at Boston and York. He was incapable of fear, meeting personal dangers with the calmest unconcern. Perhaps the strongest feature in his character was prudence, never acting until every circumstance, every consideration, was maturely weighed; refraining if he saw a doubt, but, when once decided, going through with his purpose, whatever obstacles opposed. His integrity was most pure, his justice the most inflexible I have ever known, no motives of interest or consanguinity, or friendship or hatred, being able to bias his decision. He was, indeed, in every sense of the words, a wise, a good, and a great man. His temper was naturally high toned; but reflection and resolution had obtained a firm and habitual ascendancy over it. If ever, however, it broke its bonds, he was most tremendous in his wrath. In his expenses he was honorable, but exact; liberal in contributions to whatever promised utility; but frowning and unyielding on all visionary projects and all unworthy calls on his charity. His heart was not warm in its affections; but he exactly calculated every man's value, and gave him a solid esteem proportioned to it. His person, you know, was fine, his stature exactly what one would wish, his deportment easy, erect and noble; the best horseman of his age, and the most graceful figure that could be seen on horseback. Although in the circle of his friends, where he might be unreserved with safety, he took a free share in conversation, his colloquial talents were not above mediocrity, possessing neither copiousness of ideas, nor fluency of words. In public, when called on for a sudden opinion, he was unready, short and embarrassed. Yet he wrote readily, rather diffusely, in an easy and correct style. This he had acquired by conversation with the world, for his education was merely reading, writing and common arithmetic, to which he added surveying at a later day. His time was employed in action chiefly, reading little, and only in agriculture and English history. His correspondence became necessarily extensive, and, with journalizing his agricultural proceedings, occupied most of his leisure hours within doors. On the whole, his character was, in its mass, perfect, in nothing bad, in few points indifferent; and it may truly be said, that never did nature and fortune combine more perfectly to make a man great, and to place him in the same constellation with whatever worthies have merited from man an everlasting remembrance. For his was the singular destiny and merit of leading the armies of his country successfully through an arduous war, for the establishment of its independence, of conducting its councils through the birth of a government, new in its forms and principles, until it had settled down into a quiet and orderly train; and of scrupulously obeying the laws through the whole of his career, civil and military, of which the history of the world furnishes no other example.

Thomas Jefferson to Dr. Walter Jones
1814

Rules Proper to Be Observed in Trade

-Endeavour to be perfect in the calling you are engaged in, and be assiduous in every part thereof; INDUSTRY being the natural means of acquiring wealth, honour, and reputation; as idleness is of poverty, shame, and disgrace.

-Lay a good foundation in regard to principle; Be sure not wilfully to over-reach, or deceive your neighbor; but keep always in your eye the golden rule of doing as you would be done unto.

-Be strict in discharging all legal debts: Do not evade your creditors by any shuffling arts, in giving notes under your hand, only to defer payment; but, if you have it in your power, discharge all debts when they become due. Above all, when you are straitened for lack of money, be cautious of taking it up at a high interest. This has been the ruin of many, therefore endeavour to avoid it.

-Be complacent to the least, as well as the greatest:

You are as much obliged to use good manners for a penny, as a dollar; the one demands it from you, as well as the other.

-Take great care in keeping your accounts well: Enter everything necessary in your books with neatness and exactness; often state your accounts, and examine whether you gain, or lose; and carefully survey your stock, and inspect into every particular of your affairs.

-Strive to maintain a fair character in the world: That will be the best means for advancing your credit, gaining you the most flourishing trade, and enlarging your fortune. Condescend to no mean action, but add a lustre to trade by keeping up to the dignity of your nature.

Benjamin Franklin
The Pennsylvania Gazette 1749

Rules for Making Oneself a Disagreeable Companion

Your business is to shine; therefore you must by all means prevent the shining of others, for their brightness may make yours the less distinguished. To this end,

1. If possible engross the whole discourse; and when other matter fails, talk much of yourself, your education, your knowledge, your circumstances, your successes in business, your victories in disputes, your own wise sayings and observations on particular occasions, &c. &c. &c.

2. If when you are out of breath, one of the company should seize the opportunity of saying something, watch his words, and, if possible, find something either in his sentiment or expression, immediately to contradict and raise a dispute upon. Rather than fail, criticize even his grammar.

3. If another should be saying an indisputably good thing, either give no attention to it; or interrupt him; or draw away the attention of others; or, if you can guess

what he would be at, be quick and say it before him; or if he gets it said, and you perceive the company to be pleased with it, own it to be a good thing, and remark that it had been said by Bacon, Locke, Bayle, or some other eminent writer; thus you deprive him of the reputation he might have gained by it, and gain some yourself, as you hereby show your great reading and memory.

4. When modest men have been thus treated by you a few times, they will choose ever after to be silent in your company; then you may shine on without fear of rival; rallying them at the same time for their dullness, which will be to you a new fund of wit. Thus you will be sure to please yourself. The polite man aims at pleasing others, but you shall go beyond him even in that. A man can be present only in one company, but may at the same time be absent in twenty. He can please only where he is, you wherever you are not.

Benjamin Franklin
The Pennsylvania Gazette 1750

Experience is a severe preceptor, but it teaches useful truths, and however harsh, is always honest—Be calm and dispassionate, and listen to what it tells us.

John Jay
1788

While I feel the most lively gratitude for the many instances of the approbation from my country, I cannot otherwise deserve it, than by obeying the dictates of my conscience.

George Washington
1795

Virtue and happiness are mother and daughter.

What you would seem to be, be really.

He's a fool that cannot conceal his wisdom.

Industry, perseverance and frugality make fortune yield.

Hear reason, or she'll make you feel her.

The things which hurt, instruct.

'Tis easy to frame a good, bold resolution;
but hard is the task that concerns execution.

Against diseases here, the strongest fence,
is the defensive virtue, abstinence.

Up, sluggard, and waste not life;
in the grave will be sleeping enough.

No longer virtuous no longer free; is a maxim as true
with regard to a private person as a commonwealth.

Search others for their virtues, thyself for thy vices.

As we must account for every idle word,
so we must for every idle silence.

After crosses and losses men grow humbler and wiser.

He that cannot obey, cannot command.

Innocence is its own defense.

Men take more pains to mask than to mend.

Half the truth is often a great lie.

Would you live with ease?
Do what you ought, not what you please.

If a man could have half his wishes,
he would double his troubles.

Bad gains are truly losses.

Act uprightly, and despise calumny; dirt may
stick to a mud wall, but not to polished marble.

Sell not virtue to purchase wealth,
nor liberty to purchase power.

Pain wastes the body, pleasures the understanding.

Think of three things: whence you came,
where you are, and to whom you must account.

Glass, China and reputation are easily cracked,

and never well mended.

Today is yesterday's pupil.

Many a man thinks he is buying pleasure,
when he is really selling himself a slave to it.

Wouldst thou confound thine enemy? Be good thyself.

Pardoning the bad is injuring the good.

When you're good to others, you are best to yourself.

Liberality is not giving much, but giving wisely.

There is no man so bad,
but he secretly respects the good.

Let no pleasure tempt you, no profit allure you, no
ambition corrupt you, no example sway you, no
persuasion move you, to do anything which you know
to be evil; so shall you always live jollily; for a good
conscience is a continual Christmas.

If thou injurset conscience,
it will have its revenge on thee.

No resolution of repenting hereafter, can be sincere.

You may be more happy than Princes,
if you will be more virtuous.

Buy what thou hast no need of;
and e'er long thou shalt sell thy necessaries.
Is there anything men take more pains about
than to render themselves unhappy?

The noblest question in the world is
What good may I do in it?

He that can compose himself,
is wiser than he that composes books.

At the working man's house hunger
looks in but dares not enter.

The nearest way to come at glory,
is to do that for conscience which we do for glory.

Well done is better than well said.

He that would live in peace and at ease,
Must not speak all he knows, nor judge all he sees.

Do not do that which you would not have known.

Diligence is the mother of Good-Luck.

Wealth is not his that has it, but his that enjoys it.

Don't throw stones at your neighbors,
if your own windows are glass.

He that lives well is learned enough

The excellency of hogs is fatness, of men virtue.

To be humble to superiors is duty,
to equals courtesy, to inferiors nobleness.

It is better to take many injuries than to give one.

Are you angry that others disappoint you?
Remember you cannot depend upon yourself.

If you would be revenged of your enemy,
govern your self.

He that waits upon fortune, is never sure of a dinner.

Do good to thy friend to keep him,
to thy enemy to gain him.

A good man is seldom uneasy, an ill one never easy.

Who pleasure gives, shall joy receive.

He is ill clothed, who is bare of virtue.

Benjamin Franklin
Poor Richard's Almanac 1733-1758

A wise and honest administration, may make the
people happy under any government.

Richard Henry Lee
1787

Happiness, whether in despotism or democracy, whether in slavery or liberty, can never be found without virtue.

John Adams
1787

If the people of our nation, instead of consenting to be governed by laws of their own making, and rulers of their own choosing, should let licentiousness, disorder, and confusion reign over them, the minds of men everywhere, will insensibly become alienated from republican forms, and prepared to prefer and acquiesce in governments, which, though less friendly to liberty, afford more peace and security.

John Jay
1788

More, in my opinion, is to be done than conquering our British enemies, in order to establish the liberties of our country on a solid basis...

. . . May Heaven inspire the present rulers with wisdom and sound understanding! In all probability they will stamp the character of the people. It is natural for a sensible observer to form an estimate of the people from an opinion of the men whom they set up for their legislators and magistrates. And besides, if we look into the history of governors, we shall find that their principles and manners have always had a mighty influence on the people. Should vanity and foppery ever be the ruling taste among the great, the body of the people would be in danger of catching the distemper, and the ridiculous maxims of the one would become fashionable among the other. . . .

. . . If men of wisdom and knowledge, of moderation and temperance, of patience, fortitude and perseverance, of sobriety and true republican simplicity of manners, of zeal for the honour of the Supreme Being and the welfare of the commonwealth, if men possessed of these and other excellent qualities are chosen to fill the seats of government, we may expect that our affairs will rest on a solid and permanent foundation.

Samuel Adams
1780

I go on this great republican principle, that the people will have virtue and intelligence to select men of virtue and wisdom. Is there no virtue among us? If there be not, we are in a wretched situation. No theoretical checks—no form of government can render us secure. To suppose that any form of government will secure liberty or happiness without any virtue in the people, is a chimerical idea. If there be sufficient virtue and intelligence in the community, it will be exercised in the selection of these men. So that we do not depend on their virtue, or put confidence in our rulers, but in the people who are to choose them.

James Madison
1788

It is much safer to follow truth alone, than to have all the world for company in the road of error; Therefore when sinners entice, consent thou not . . . A fiction may be clothed with probability, and the disguise of truth become a passport for a mischievous lie. The grossest story, when artificially cooked by cunning envy, may appear likely, and gain belief. A seeming reason, be disguised and veiled for a season; Yet like the sun in the firmament, whose glory is often eclipsed by the interception of his rays, he does by the efflux of his own light, dispel the mist, and leave his native beauty unblemished, so shall truth rise upon falsehood.

Nathaniel Greene to Samuel Ward, Jr.
1771

Sir: You will observe that on the arrangement of the officers attested to New York there is an alternative of Wm. S. Smith or Abijah Hammond for Lt Colonel Commandant. Various considerations demand that the motive of his hesitation should be explained. Had military qualifications alone been consulted, the name of Colonel Smith would have stood justly and he would have been deemed a valuable acquisition to the service. Had there even been no other source of objection than the erroneous political opinions of late attributed to him, his honour and attachment to his country would have been relied upon. But as well myself as the two generals whose aid I have had in the nominations have been afflicted with the information well or ill founded that he stands charged in the opinion of his fellow citizens with very serious instances of private misconduct; instances which affect directly his integrity as a man. The instances alleged are various, but there is one which has come forward in a shape which did not permit us to refuse it our attention. It respects an attempt knowingly to pledge property to Major Burrows by way of security, which was before conveyed or mortgaged for its full value to Mr. William Constable; without giving notice of the circumstances, and with the aggravation, that Major Burrows had become the creditor of Col Smith through friendship to an amount which has proved entirely ruinous to him. While the impossibility of disregarding this information forbade the selection of Col Smith absolutely, the possibility that it might admit of some fair explanation dissuaded from a conclusion against him. As it will be in your power to obtain further lights on the subject, it has appeared advisable to leave the matter in the undetermined form in which it is presented and to assign the reason first.

George Washington to the Secretary of War
1798

If ever you are about to say anything amiss or to do anything wrong, consider beforehand. You will feel something within you which will tell you it is wrong and ought not to be said or done; this is your conscience, and be sure to obey it. Our Maker has given us all this faithful internal Monitor, and if you always obey it, you will always be prepared for the end of the world; or for a much more certain event which is death. This must happen to all; it puts an end to the world as to us.

Thomas Jefferson to Martha Jefferson
1783

Youth is most certainly a time of innocence when we have horror for vice; which we never commit at first without doing violence to our nature. How our soul startles when we attempt to perpetrate a crime prohibited by laws both human and divine!

Nathaniel Greene to Samuel Ward, Jr.
1772

A man remarkably wavering and inconstant, who . . . adheres to no purpose that he has resolved on, whose courage is surmounted by the most trifling obstacles, whose judgement is at any time bypassed by his fears, whose trembling and disturbed imagination will at every turn suggest to him difficulties and dangers that actually have no existence, and enlarge those that have; A man, I say, of this stamp, whatever natural and acquired qualities he may have, can never be a truly useful member of a commonwealth, a sincere or amiable friend, or a formidable enemy.

Benjamin Franklin
1734

Honesty, sincerity, and openness I esteem essential marks of a good mind. I am therefore, of opinion that men ought . . . to avow their opinions and defend them with boldness.

John Adams
Diary 1756

THE WAY TO WEALTH

I have heard that nothing gives an author so great pleasure as to find his works respectfully quoted by others. Judge, then, how much I must have been gratified by an incident I am going to relate to you. I stopped my horse lately where a great number of people were collected at an auction of merchants' goods. The hour of the sale not being come, they were conversing on the badness of the times; and one of the company called to a plain, clean old man, with white locks, "Pray, Father Abraham, what think you of the times? Will not those heavy taxes quite ruin the country? How shall we ever be able to pay them? What would you advise us to?" Father Abraham stood up, and replied, "If you would have my advice, I will give it you in short, 'for a word to the wise is enough,' as Poor Richard says." They joined in desiring him to speak his mind and gathering round him, he proceeded as follows:

"Friends," says he, "the taxes are, indeed, very heavy, and, if those laid on by the government were the only ones he had to pay, we might more easily discharge them; but we have many others, and much more grievous to some of us. We are taxed twice as much by our idleness, three times as much by our pride, and four times as much by our folly; and from these taxes the commissioners cannot ease or deliver us by allowing an abatement. However, let us hearken to good advice, and something may be done for us; 'God helps them that help themselves,' as Poor Richard says.

"It would be thought a hard government that should tax its people one-tenth part of their time, to be employed in its service, but idleness taxes many of us much more, sloth, by bringing on diseases, absolutely shortens life, 'Sloth, like rust, consumes faster than labor wears, while the used key is always bright,' as Poor Richard says. 'But dost thou love life, then do not squander time, for that is the stuff life is made of,' as Poor Richard says. How much more than is necessary do we spend in sleep, forgetting that 'the sleeping fox catches no poultry, and that there will be sleeping enough in the grave,' as Poor Richard says.

" 'If time be of all things the most precious, wasting time must be,' as Poor Richard says, 'the greatest prodigality,' since, as he elsewhere tells us, 'lost time is never found again; and what we call time enough always proves little enough.' Let us then up and be doing, and doing to the purpose, so by diligence shall we do more with less perplexity. 'Sloth makes all things difficult, but industry all easy; and he that riseth late must trot all day and shall scarce overtake his business at night; while laziness travels so slowly that poverty soon overtakes him. Drive thy business, let not that drive thee; and early to bed and early to rise, makes a man healthy, wealthy, and wise,' as Poor Richard says.

"So what signifies wishing and hoping for better times? We may make these times better if we bestir ourselves. 'Industry need not wish, and he that lives upon hope will die fasting. There are no gains without pains; then help hands for I have no lands.' Or, if I have, they are smartly taxed. 'He that hath a trade, hath an estate; and he that hath a calling, hath an office of profit and honour,' as Poor Richard says. But then the trade must be worked at, and the calling well followed, or neither the estate nor the office will enable us to pay our taxes. If we are industrious, we shall never starve; for, 'at the workingman's house, hunger looks in but dares not enter.' Nor will the bailiff or the constable enter, for 'industry pays debts, while despair increaseth them.'

"What though you have found no treasure, nor has any rich relation left you a legacy, 'diligence is the mother of good luck, and God gives all things to industry. Then plow deep, while sluggards sleep, and you shall have corn to sell and to keep.' Work while it is called today, for you know not how much you may be hindered tomorrow. 'One today is worth two tomorrows,' as Poor Richard says; and further, 'never leave that till tomorrow which you can do today.'

"If you were a servant, would you not be ashamed that a good master should catch you idle? Are you then your own master? Be ashamed to catch yourself idle when there is so much to be done for yourself, your family, your country, and your king. Handle your tools without mittens; remember that the cat in gloves catches no mice,' as Poor Richard says. It is true, there is much to be done, and perhaps you are weak-handed; but stick to it steadily, and you will see great effects, for 'constant dripping wears away stones; and by diligence and patience the mouse ate in two the cable; and little strokes fell great oaks.'

"Methinks I hear some of you say, 'must a man afford himself no leisure?' I will tell thee, my friend, what Poor Richard says: 'Employ thy time well, if thou meanest to gain leisure; and since thou art not sure of a minute, throw not away an hour.' Leisure is time for doing something useful; this leisure the diligent man will obtain, but the lazy man never; for a life of leisure and a life of laziness are two different things. Many, without labor, would live by their wits only, but they break for want of stock'; whereas industry gives comfort and plenty and respect. 'Fly pleasures, and they will follow you. The diligent spinner has a large shift; and now I have a sheep and a cow, everybody bids me goodmorrow.'

"But with our industry we must likewise be steady, settled, and careful, and oversee our own affairs with our own eyes, and not trust too much to others; for, as Poor Richard says,

I never saw an oft-removed tree.
Nor yet an oft-removed family,
That throve so well as those that settled be.

"And again, 'Three removes is as bad as a fire'; and again, 'Keep thy shop, and thy shop will keep thee'; and again, 'If you would have your business done, go, if not, send'; and again, 'He that by the plow would thrive, himself must either hold or drive. "And again, 'The eye of a master will do more work than both his hands'; and again, 'Want of care does us more damage than want of knowledge'; and again, 'Not to oversee workmen is to leave them your purse open.' Trusting too much to others' care is the ruin of many; for, 'in the affairs of this world, men are saved, not by faith but by the want of it.' But a man's own care is profitable, for, ' if you would have a faithful servant, and one that you like, serve yourself. A little neglect may breed great mischief; for want of a nail the shoe was lost, and for want of a shoe the horse was lost, and for want of a horse the rider was lost,' being overtaken and slain by the enemy; all for want of a little care about a horseshoe nail.

"So much for industry, my friends, and attention to one's own business; but to these we must add frugality, if we would make our industry more certainly successful. A man may, if he knows not how to save as he gets, 'keep his nose all his life to the grindstone and die not worth a groat at last. A fat kitchen makes a lean will'; and,

　　　Many estates are spent in the getting,
Since women for tea forsook spinning and knitting,
And men for punch forsook hewing and splitting.

"If you would be wealthy, think of saving as well as of getting. The Indies have not made Spain rich, because her outgoes are greater than her incomes.

"Away, then, with your expensive follies, and you will not then have so much cause to complain of hard times, heavy taxes, and chargeable families; for

　　　Women and wine, game and deceit,
　　Make the wealth small, and the want great.

"And further, 'What maintains one vice, would bring up two children.' You may think, perhaps, that a little tea, or a little punch now and then, diet a little more costly, clothes a little finer, and a little entertainment now and then can be no great matter; but remember, 'Many a little makes a nickel.' Beware of little expenses; 'A small leak will sink a great ship,' as Poor Richard says; and again, 'Who dainties love shall beggars prove'; and moreover, 'Fools make feasts, and wise men eat them.'

"Here you are all got together to this sale of fineries and knickknacks. You call them goods, but if you do not take care, they will prove evils to some of you. You expect they will be sold cheap, and perhaps they may, for less than they cost; but, if you have no occasion for them, they must be dear to you. Remember what Poor Richard says, 'Buy what thou hast no need of, and ere long thou shalt sell thy necessaries.' And again, 'At a great pennyworth pause a while.' He means that perhaps the cheapness is apparent only, and not real; or the bargain, by straitening thee in thy business, may do thee more harm than good. For in another place he says, 'Many have been ruined by buying good pennyworths.' Again, 'It is foolish to lay out money in a purchase of repentance'; and yet this folly is practiced everyday at auctions, for want of minding the Almanac.

"Many a one, for the sake of finery on the back, have gone with a hungry belly, and half-starved their families; 'Silks and satins, scarlet and velvets, put out the kitchen fire,' as Poor Richard says. These are not the necessaries of life, they can scarcely be called the conveniences; and yet, only because they look pretty, how many want to have them? By these and other extravagances, the genteel are reduced to poverty, and forced to borrow of those whom they formerly despised, but who, through industry and frugality, have maintained their standing; in which case it appears plainly, that 'a plowman on his legs is higher than a gentleman on his knees,' as Poor Richard says.

"Perhaps they have had a small estate left them, which they knew not the getting of; they think 'it is day and will never be night', that a little to be spent out of so much is not worth minding; but 'always taking out of the meal tub, and never putting in, soon comes to the bottom,' as Poor Richard says; and then, when the well is dry, they know the worth of water. But this they might have known before, if they had taken his advice: 'If you would know the value of money go and try to borrow some; for he that goes a-borrowing goes a-sorrowing,' as Poor Richard says; and, indeed, so does he that lends to such people, when he goes to get it in again. Poor Dick further advises and says,

> Fond pride of dress is sure a very curse,
> Ere fancy you consult, consult your purse.

"And again, 'Pride is as loud a beggar as want, and a great deal more saucy.' When you have bought one fine thing, you must buy ten more that your appearance may be all of a piece; but Poor Dick says, 'It is easier to suppress the first desire than to satisfy all that follow it'; and it is as truly folly for the poor to ape the rich as for the frog to swell in order to equal the ox.

> Vessels large may venture more,
> But little boats should keep near shore.

"It is, however, a folly soon punished; for, as Poor Richard says, 'Pride that dines on vanity, sups on contempt; pride breakfasted with plenty, dined with poverty, and supped with infamy.' And, after all, of what use is this pride of appearance, for which so much is risked, so much is suffered? It cannot promote health, nor ease pain; it makes no increase of merit in the person; it creates envy; it hastens misfortune.

"But what madness must it be to run in debt for these superfluities! We are offered, by the terms of this sale, six-months credit; and that, perhaps, has induced some of us to attend it, because we cannot spare the ready money and hope now to be fine without it. But, ah! think what you do when you run in debt; you give to another power over your liberty. If you cannot pay at the time, you will be ashamed to see your creditor; you will be in fear when you speak to him; you will make poor pitiful sneaking excuses and, by degrees, come to lose your veracity and sink into base, downright lying; for, 'the second vice is lying, the first is running in debt,' as Poor Richard says; and again, to the same purpose, 'lying rides upon debt's back'; whereas a freeborn Englishman ought not to be ashamed nor afraid to see or speak to any man living. But poverty often deprives a man of all spirit and virtue. 'It is hard for an empty bag to stand upright.'

"What would you think of that prince, or of that government, who should issue an edict forbidding you to dress like a gentleman or gentlewoman, on pain of imprisonment or servitude? Would you not say that you were free, have a right to dress as you please, and that such an edict would be a breach of your privileges, and such a government tyrannical? And yet you are about to put yourself under that tyranny, when you run in debt for such dress! Your creditor has authority, at his pleasure, to deprive you of your liberty by confining you in jail for life, or by selling you for a servant, if you should not be able to pay him.

"When you have got your bargain, you may, perhaps, think little of payment; but, as Poor Richard says, 'Creditors have better memories than debtors; creditors are a superstitious sect, great observers of set days and times.' The day comes round before you are aware, and the demand is made before you are prepared to satisfy it; or, if you bear your debt in mind, the term, which at first seemed so long, will, as it lessens, appear extremely short—time will seem to have added wings to his heels as well as his shoulders. 'Those have a short Lent who owe money to be paid at Easter.' At present, perhaps, you may think yourselves in thriving circumstances, and that you can bear a little extravagance without injury; but

> For age and want save while you may,
> No morning sun lasts a whole day.

"Gain may be temporary and uncertain, but ever, while you live, expense is constant and certain; and, 'it

is easier to build two chimneys that to keep one in fuel,'
as Poor Richard says; so 'rather go to bed supperless
than rise in debt.'

> Get what you can, and what you get hold,
> 'Tis the stone that will turn all your lead into gold.

"And when you have got the philosopher's stone,
sure you will no longer complain of bad times, or the
difficulty of paying taxes.

"This doctrine, my friends, is reason and wisdom;
but, after all, do not depend too much upon your own
industry and frugality and prudence, though excellent
things; for they may all be blasted, without the blessing
of heaven. And, therefore, ask that blessing humbly,
and be not uncharitable to those that at present seem to
want it, but comfort and help them. Remember Job
suffered and was afterward prosperous.

"And now, to conclude, 'experience keeps a dear
school, but fools will learn in no other,' as Poor Richard
says, and scarce in that; for, it is true, 'We may give
advice, but we cannot give conduct'; however, remember this, 'They that will not be counseled cannot be
helped'; and further, that 'if you will not hear reason
she will surely rap your knuckles,' as Poor Richard says."

Thus the old gentleman ended his harangue. The
people heard it and approved the doctrine and immediately practiced the contrary, just as if it had been a
common sermon; for the auction opened and they began to buy extravagantly.

I found the good man had thoroughly studied my
almanacs and digested all I had dropped on those topics during the course of twenty-five years. The frequent
mention he made of me must have tired anyone else;
but my vanity was wonderfully delighted with it, though
I was conscious that not a tenth part of the wisdom was
my own, which he ascribed to me but rather the glean-
ings that I had made of the sense of all ages and nations. However, I resolved to be the better for the echo
of it; and, though I had at first determined to buy stuff

for a new coat, I went away, resolved to wear my old one a little longer. Reader, if thou wilt do the same, thy profit will be as great as mine.

Benjamin Franklin
Poor Richard's Almanac 1758

. . . Diligence, frugality, and integrity will infallibly increase your business, and your fortunes. If you can content yourself with moderate things at first, you will rise, perhaps, by slow degrees, but upon a solid and safe foundation.

George Mason to son John
1788

You may be assured that there is no practice more dangerous than that of borrowing money . . . for when money can be had in this way, repayment is seldom thought of in time; the interest becomes a moth . . . exertions to raise it by dint of industry ceases— it comes easy and is spent freely—in the meantime the debt in accumulating like a snowball in rolling.

George Washington to Samuel Washington
1797

The foundation of our national policy will be laid in the pure and immutable principle of private morality . . . since there is no truth more thoroughly established than that there exists in the economy and course of nature an indissoluble union between virtue and happiness; between duty and advantage; between the genuine maxims of an honest and magnanimous policy and the solid rewards of public prosperity and felicity; since we ought to be no less persuaded that the propitious smiles of Heaven can never be expected on a nation that disregards the eternal rules of order and right which Heaven itself has ordained.

George Washington
1st Inaugural Address 1789

What virtue above all others would a good man wish to be generally known by the world and by posterity? I should suppose integrity.

Benjamin Rush to John Adams

I sincerely pray that my mind may be never tainted with the base ambition of rising by sordid practices. No dignities can adorn his character, who has attained them by meanness. With equal scorn do I behold him, who endeavours to recommend himself, either to men of power, or to the public, by flattering their passions or errors, and by forfeiting his honour and integrity.

The good man who is guided through life by his conscience and reason, may in particular instances, offend even honest and wise men—but his virtue will naturally produce a uniformity in his conduct upon the whole, that will discover his probity, and procure him the general approbation of the worthy.

John Dickinson
1764

There is a natural aristocracy among men. The grounds of this are virtue and talent.

Thomas Jefferson to John Adams
1813

Virtue is not always amiable.

John Adams
Diary 1779

Frequent recurrence to fundamental principles, and a firm adherence to justice, moderation, temperance, industry, and frugality are absolutely necessary to preserve the blessings of liberty, and keep government free. The people ought, therefore, to pay particular attention to these points, in the choice of officers and representatives, and have a right to exact a due and constant regard to them, from their legislators and magistrates, in the making and executing such laws as are necessary for the good government of the state.

from the Constitution of Vermont
1777

Your affectionate and excellent father has requested that I would address to you something which might possibly have a favorable influence on the course of life you have to run, and I too, as a namesake, feel an interest in that course. Few words will be necessary, with good dispositions on your part. Adore God. Reverence and cherish your parents. Love your neighbor as yourself, and your country more than yourself. Be just. Be true. Murmur not at the ways of Providence.

Thomas Jefferson to Thomas Jefferson Smith
1825

Some states have lost their liberty by particular accidents: But this calamity is generally owing to the decay of virtue. A people is travelling fast to destruction, when individuals consider their interests as distinct from those of the public. Such notions are fatal to their country, and to themselves. Yet how many are there, so weak and sordid as to think they perform all the offices of life, if they earnestly endeavour to increase their own wealth, power, and credit, without the least regard for the society, under the protection of which they live; who, if they can make an immediate profit to themselves, by lending their assistance to those, whose projects plainly tend to the injury of their country, rejoice in their dexterity, and believe themselves entitled to the character of able politicians. Miserable men! Of whom it is hard to say, whether they ought to be most the objects of pity or contempt: But whose opinions are certainly as detestable as their practices are destructive.

John Dickinson

Much of the strength and efficiency of any government, in procuring and securing happiness to the people, depends on opinion, on the general opinion of the goodness of that government, as well as of the wisdom and integrity of its governors.

Benjamin Franklin
1787

The whole art of government consists in the art of being honest. Only aim to do your duty, and mankind will give you credit where you fail. No longer persevere in sacrificing the rights of one part of the empire to the inordinate desires of another; but deal out to all equal and impartial right.

Thomas Jefferson
A Summary View of the Rights of
British America 1774

My principle is to do whatever is right, and leave the consequences to Him who has the disposal of them.

Thomas Jefferson to James Martin
1813

I hope I shall always possess firmness and virtue enough to maintain (what I consider the most enviable of all titles) the character of an honest man.

George Washington to Alexander Hamilton
1788

If you would know any man's affection towards you, consult his behavior; that is the best evidence of a virtuous mind. Though a person's professions be ever so voluminous, and his zeal ever so noisy, yet he is not entitled to our esteem, but only civility; for profession is but the shadow of friendship, and saying is not proving. If a person would be considered in the character of a friend, let it appear by generous and friendly actions; for that is the only testimony upon which we may safely ground our esteem. If a man professes friendship one day and proves himself an enemy the next, why should I give credit to one who so effectually contradicts himself. Why should we trust any man's professions before he has proved them to be sincere by noble and generous actions?

Nathaniel Greene to Samuel Ward Jr.
1772

Friendship like all truth delights in plainness and simplicity, and it is the counterfeit alone that needs ornament and ostentation. I am so thoroughly persuaded of this that when I observe anyone over complaisant to me in his professions and promises, I am tempted to interpret his language thus: As I have no real esteem for you, and for certain reasons think it expedient to appear well in your eye, I endeavour to varnish falsehood with politeness, which I think I can do in so ingenious a manner that so vain a blockhead as you cannot see through it.

James Madison to William Bradford
1773

Power, grandeur, and prosperity mingle an intoxi-
cating draught, generally too strong for the limited understanding and fallible virtue of mortality. We are not
forming plans for a day, month, year, or age, but for
eternity. Let us endeavour with united councils to establish a government that not only may render our nation
great, respectable, free, and happy, but also VIRTU-
OUS. Let us try to combine political establishments with
moral virtue that if possible the first may be equal with
the duration of this world and an aid or at least not a
hindrance to the enjoyment of another.

John Dickinson
Constitutional Convention 1787

I believe, with you, that a republican government,
while the people have the virtues, talents, and love of
country necessary to support it, the best possible government to promote the interest, dignity, and happiness
of man.

John Adams to Benjamin Rush
1808

A popular government is the worst curse to which
human nature can be devoted, when it is thoroughly
corrupted. Despotism is better. A sober, conscientious
habit of electing for the public good alone must be introduced, and every appearance of interest, favor, and
partiality condemned, or you will very soon make wise
and honest men wish for monarchy again; nay, you will
make them introduce it into America.

John Adams to Joseph Hawley
1776

The aim of every political Constitution is or ought
to be first to obtain for rulers, men who possess most

wisdom to discern, and most virtue to pursue the common good of the society . . .

James Madison
The Federalist #57 1788

But let it be remembered that whatever marks of wisdom, experience and patriotism there may be in your constitution, yet like the beautiful symmetry, the just proportions, and elegant forms of our first parents, before their Maker breathed into them the breath of life, it is yet to be animated, and till then, may indeed excite admiration, but will be of no use—from the people it must receive its spirit, and by them be quickened. Let virtue, honour, the love of liberty and of science be, and remain, the soul of this constitution, and it will become the source of great extensive happiness to this and future generations. Vice, ignorance, and want of vigilance, will be the only enemies able to destroy it. Against these provide, and, of these, be forever jealous.

John Jay
1777

There is an option still left to the United States of America, it is in their choice and depends upon their conduct, whether they will be respectable and prosperous, or contemptible and miserable as a nation.

George Washington to the Governors
1783

Yes, we did produce a near perfect Republic. But will they keep it, or will they, in the enjoyment of plenty, lose the memory of freedom? Material abundance without character is the surest way to destruction.

Thomas Jefferson

Arbitrary power is most easily established on the ruins of liberty abused to licentiousness.

George Washington
Farewell Address 1796

I have always concurred in the general principle that the industrious pursuits of individuals ought to be left to individuals, as most capable of choosing and managing them. And this policy is certainly most congenial with the spirit of a free people, and is particularly due to the intelligent and enterprising citizens of the United States.

James Madison
1824

Well, my friend, thou art now just entering the last month of another year. If thou art a man of business, and of prudent care, belike thou wilt now settle thy accounts, to satisfy thyself whether thou hast gained or lost in the year past, and how much of either, the better to regulate thy future industry or thy common expenses. This is commendable—But it is not all—Wilt thou not examine also thy moral accounts, and see what improvements thou has made in the conduct of life, what vice subdued, what virtue acquired; how much better and wiser, as well as how much richer thou art grown? What shall it profit a man, if he gain the whole world, and lose his own soul? Without some care in this matter, tho' thou may'st come to count thy thousands, thou wilt possibly still appear poor in the eyes of the discerning, even here, and be really so for ever hereafter.

Benjamin Franklin
Poor Richard's Almanac 1756

2

Patriotism

"-And for the support of this
Declaration . . .
we mutually pledge to each other
our lives,
our fortunes and our sacred honor."

"My affections are deeply rooted in America..." wrote John Jay to Gouverneur Morris from France, *"... I can never become so far a citizen of the world as to view every part of it with equal regard."* About a century later, Theodore Roosevelt expressed similar sentiments. *"The man who loves other countries,"* he said, *"as much as his own, stands on a level with the man who loves other women as much as he loves his own wife."*

By today's standards, Chief Justice Jay and President Roosevelt would likely be scorned by those who dismiss patriotism as active rebellion to the international community.

In this day of global awareness, should we not consider this prophecy made in 1808 by John Adams?

"When public virtue is gone, when the national spirit is fled ... the republic is lost in essence, though it may still exist in form."

Posterity! You will never know how much it cost the present generation to preserve your freedom! I hope you will make good use of it! If you do not, I shall repent it in heaven that I ever took half the pains to preserve it!

John Adams to Abigail Adams
1777

Observe that if your cause is just, if your principles are pure, and if your conduct is prudent, you need not fear the multitude of opposing hosts.

John Witherspoon

There are certain maxims by which every wise and enlightened people will regulate their conduct. There are certain political maxims, which no free people ought ever to abandon. Maxims of which the observance is essential to the security of happiness. It is impiously irritating the avenging hand of Heaven, when a people who are in the full enjoyment of freedom, launch out into the wide ocean of human affairs, and desert those maxims which alone can preserve liberty. Such maxims, humble as they are, are those only which can render a nation safe or formidable. Poor little humble republican maxims have attracted the admiration and engaged the attention of the virtuous and wise in all nations, and have stood the shock of ages. We do not now admit the validity of maxims, which we once delighted in. We have since adopted maxims of a different but more refined nature: New maxims which tend to the prostration of republicanism.

We have one, Sir, That all men are by nature free and independent, and have certain inherent rights, of which, when they enter into society, they cannot by any compact deprive or divest their posterity. We have a set of maxims of the same spirit, which must be beloved by

every friend to liberty, to virtue, to mankind. Our Bill of
Rights contains those admirable maxims.

Patrick Henry to Edmund Randolph
1788

. . . It is unquestionably true that the great body of
the people love their country and wish it prosperity; and
this observation is particularly applicable to the people
of a free country, for they have more and stronger reasons for loving it than others.

John Jay
Address to the People of New York 1787

In the fall of 1774 and winter of 1775, I was one of
upwards of thirty, chiefly mechanics, who formed ourselves into a committee for the purpose of watching the
movements of the British soldiers, and gaining every
intelligence of the movements of the Tories. We held
our meeting at the Green Dragon tavern. We were so
careful that our meetings should be kept secret that
every time we met, every person swore upon the Bible
that they would not discover any of our transactions but
to Messrs. Hancock, Adams, Doctors Warren, Church
and one or two more.

. . . In the winter, towards the spring, we frequently
took turns, two and two, to watch the soldiers by patrol-
ling the streets all night. The Saturday night preceding
the 19th of April, about 12 o'clock at night, the boats
belonging to the transports were all launched and carried under the sterns of the men-of-war. (They had been
previously hauled up and repaired.) We likewise found
that the grenadiers and light infantry were all taken off
duty.

From these movements we expected something serious was to be transacted. On Tuesday evening, the
18th, it was observed that a number of soldiers were
marching towards the bottom of the Common. About 10

o'clock, Dr. Warren sent in great haste for me and begged that I would immediately set off for Lexington, where Messrs. Hancock and Adams were, and acquaint them of the movement, and that it was thought they were the objects.

When I got to Dr. Warren's house, I found he had sent an express by land to Lexington—a Mr. William Daws. The Sunday before, by desire of Dr. Warren, I had been to Lexington, to Messrs. Hancock and Adams, who were at the Rev. Mr. Clark's. I returned at night through Charlestown; there I agreed with a Colonel Conant and some other gentlemen that if the British went out by water, we should show two lanthorns in the North Church steeple; and if by land, one, as a signal; for we were apprehensive it would be difficult to cross the Charles River or get over Boston Neck. I left Dr. Warren, called upon a friend and desired him to make the signals.

I then went home, took my boots and coat, went to the north part of the town, where I had kept a boat; two friends rowed me across Charles River, a little to the eastward where the Somerset man-of-war lay. It was then young flood, the ship was winding, and the moon was rising. They landed me on the Charlestown side. When I got into town, I met Colonel Conant and several others; they said they had seen our signals. I told them what was acting, and went to get me a horse; I got a horse of Deacon Larkin. While the horse was preparing, Richard Devens, Esq., who was one of the Committee of Safety, came to me and told me that he came down the road from Lexington after sundown that evening; that he met ten British officers, all well mounted, and armed, going up the road.

I set off upon a very good horse; it was then about eleven o'clock and very pleasant. After I had passed Charlestown Neck . . . I saw two men on horseback under a tree. When I got near them, I discovered they were British officers. One tried to get ahead of me, and the other to take me. I turned my horse very quick and galloped toward Charlestown Neck, and then pushed for the Medford Road. The one who chased me, endeavoring to cut me off, got into a clay pond near where Mr. Russell's Tavern is now built. I got clear of him, and went through Medford, over the bridge and up to Menotomy. In Medford, I awaked the captain of the minute men; and after that, I alarmed almost every house, till I got to Lexington. I found Messrs. Hancock and Adams at the Rev. Mr. Clark's; I told them my errand and enquired for Mr. Daws; they said he had not been there; I related the story of the two officers, and supposed that he must have been stopped, as he ought to have been there before me.

After I had been there about half an hour, Mr. Daws came; we refreshed ourselves, and set off for Concord. We were overtaken by a young Dr. Prescott, whom we found to be a high Son of Liberty. I told them of the ten officers that Mr. Devens met, and that it was probable we might be stopped before we got to Concord; for I supposed that after night they divided themselves, and that two of them had fixed themselves in such passages as were most likely to stop any intelligence going to Concord. I likewise mentioned that we had better alarm all the inhabitants till we got to Concord. The young doctor much approved of it and said he would stop with either of us, for the people between that and Concord knew him and would give the more credit to what we said.

We had got nearly half way. Mr. Daws and the doctor stopped to alarm the people of a house. I was about one hundred rods ahead when I saw two men in nearly the same situation as those officers were near Charlestown. I called for the doctor and Mr. Daws to come up. In an instant I was surrounded by four. They had placed themselves in a straight road that inclined each way; they had taken down a pair of bars on the north side of the road, and two of them were under a tree in the pasture. The doctor being foremost, he came up and we tried to get past them; but they being armed with pistols and swords, they forced us into the pasture.

The doctor jumped his horse over a low stone wall and got to Concord.

I observed a wood at a small distance and made for that. When I got there, out started six officers on horseback and ordered me to dismount. One of them, who appeared to have the command, examined me, where I came from and what my name was. I told him. He asked me if I was an express. I answered in the affirmative. He demanded what time I left Boston. I told him, and added that their troops had catched aground in passing the river, and that there would be five hundred Americans there in a short time, for I had alarmed the country all the way up. He immediately rode towards those who stopped us, when all five of them came down upon a full gallop. One of them, whom I afterwards found to be a Major Mitchel, of the 5th Regiment, clapped his pistol to my head, called me by name and told me he was going to ask me some questions, and if I did not give him true answers, he would blow my brains out. He then asked me similar questions to those above. He ordered them to advance and to lead me in front. When we got to the road, they turned down towards Lexington. When we had got about one mile, the major rode up to the officer that was leading me, and told him to give me to the sergeant. As soon as he took me, the major ordered him, if I attempted to run or anybody insulted them, to blow my brains out.

We rode till we got near Lexington meeting-house, when the militia fired a volley of guns, which appeared to alarm them very much. The major inquired of me how far it was to Cambridge, and if there were any other road. After some consultation, the major rode up to the sergeant and asked if his horse was tired. He answered him he was—he was a sergeant of grenadiers and had a small horse. "Then," said he, "take that man's horse." I dismounted, and the sergeant mounted my horse, when they all rode towards Lexinton meeting-house.

I went across the burying-ground and some pastures and came to the Rev. Mr. Clark's house, where I found

Messrs. Hancock and Adams. I told them of my treatment, and they concluded to go from the house towards
Woburn. I went with them and a Mr. Lowell, who was a
clerk to Mr. Hancock.

When we got to the house where they intended to
stop, Mr. Lowell and myself returned to Mr. Clark's to
find what was going on. When we got there, an elderly
man came in; he said he had just come from the tavern,
that a man had come from Boston who said there were
no British troops coming. Mr Lowell and myself went
towards the tavern, when we met a man on a full gallop,
who told us the troops were coming up the rocks. We
afterwards met another, who said they were close by. Mr
Lowell asked me to go to the tavern with him, to get a
trunk of papers belonging to Mr. Hancock. We went up
chamber, and while we were getting the trunk, we saw
the British very near, upon a full march. We hurried
towards Mr. Clark's house. In our way we passed through
the militia. There were about fifty. When we had got
about one hundred yards from the meeting-house, the
British troops appeared on both sides of the meeting-
house. In their front was an officer on horseback. They
made a short halt; when I saw, and heard, a gun fired,
which appeared to be a pistol. Then I could distinguish
two guns, and then a continual roar of musketry; when
we made off with the trunk.

Paul Revere to Dr. Jeremy Belknap
1798

Before God, I believe the hour has come. My judgment approves this measure, and my whole heart is in
it. All that I have, and all that I am, and all that I hope
in this life, I am now ready here to stake upon it. And
I leave off as I began, that live or die, survive or perish,
I am for the Declaration. It is my living sentiment, and
by the blessing of God it shall be my dying sentiment,
Independence now, and Independence forever!

John Adams
1776

Our forefathers passed the vast Atlantic, spent their blood and treasure, that they might enjoy their liberties, both civil and religious, and transmit them to their posterity. Their children have waded through seas of difficulty, to leave us free and happy in the enjoyment of English privileges. Now if we should give them up, can our children rise up and call us blessed? . . . Let us all be of one heart, and stand fast in the liberty wherewith Christ has made us free. And may He, of His infinite mercy, grant us deliverance out of all our troubles.

William Prescott

Permit me, then, to recommend from the sincerity of my heart, ready at all times to bleed in my country's cause, a declaration of independence; and call upon the world, and the great God who governs it, to witness the necessity, propriety and rectitude thereof.
. . . How will posterity, millions yet unborn, bless the memory of those brave patriots who are now hastening the consummation of Freedom, Truth, and Religion! . . . How can we, then, startle at the idea of expense, when our whole property, our dearest connections, our liberty, nay! life itself is at stake? Let us, therefore, act like men inspired with a resolution that nothing but the frowns of Heaven shall conquer us.

Nathaniel Greene to Samuel Ward
1776

"Free America"

That seat of science, Athens,
And earth's proud mistress, Rome;
Where now are all their glories?
We scarce can find a tomb.
Then guard your rights, Americans,
Nor stoop to lawless sway;
Oppose, oppose, oppose, oppose,
For North America.

Lift up your hands, ye heroes,
And swear with proud disdain,
The wretch that would ensnare you
Shall lay his snares in vain:
Should Europe empty all her force,
We'll meet her in array,
And fight and shout, and shout and fight
For North America.

Some future day shall crown us
The masters of the main,
Our fleets shall speak in thunder
To England, France and Spain;
And the nations over the ocean spread
Shall tremble and obey
The sons, the sons, the sons, the sons
Of brave America.

Joseph Warren
1774

Ever since I arrived to a state of manhood and acquainted myself with the general history of mankind, I have felt a sincere passion for liberty. The history of nations doomed to perpetual slavery, in consequence of yielding up to tyrants their natural born liberties, I read with a sort of philosophical horror; so that the first systematical and bloody attempt at Lexington to enslave America thoroughly electrified my mind and fully determined me to take part with my country.

Ethan Allen
1779

Liberty and order will never be perfectly safe until a trespass on the constitutional provisions for either, shall be felt with the same keenness that resents an invasion of the dearest rights.

James Madison
Speech to Congress 1792

A little reflection may . . . lead us to inquire whether there is not some pervading principle in Republican governments which sets at naught, and tramples upon (the) boasted superiority (of most monarchies), which have been imprudent enough to invade or attack their republican neighbors. This invincible principle is to be found in the love, the affection, the attachment of the citizens to their laws, to their freedom, and to their country—Every husbandman will be quickly converted into a soldier, when he knows and feels that he is to fight not in defense of the rights of a particular family, or a prince; but for his own. This is (what) . . . in all ages, performed such wonders—It was this which, in ancient times, enabled the little cluster of Grecian Republics to resist, and almost constantly to defeat the Persian Monarch—It was this which supported the States of Holland against a body of veteran troops thro' a thirty Years War with Spain, then the greatest Monarchy in Europe, and finally rendered them victorious.—It is this which preserves the freedom and independence of the Swiss Cantons in the midst of the most powerful nations—And who that reflects seriously upon the situation of America, in the beginning of the late war—without arms—without soldiers—without trade, money, or credit—in a manner destitute of all resources, but must ascribe our success to this pervading, all powerful principle?

George Mason
Constitutional Convention 1787

The name of AMERICAN, which belongs to you, in your national capacity, must always exalt the just pride of patriotism . . . You have in a common cause fought and triumphed together. The independence and liberty you possess are the work of joint councils, and joint efforts, of common dangers, sufferings and successes.

George Washington
Farewell Address 1796

Our unalterable resolution should be to be free.

Samuel Adams to James Warren
1776

A perpetual jealousy, respecting liberty, is absolutely requisite in all free states.

John Dickinson
Letters from a Farmer in Pennsylvania #9 1768

There must be a positive passion for the public good, the public interest, honour, power and glory, established in the minds of the people, or there can be no republican government, nor any real liberty: and this public passion must be superior to all private passions. Men must be ready, they must pride themselves and be happy to sacrifice their private pleasures, passions and interests, nay, their private friendships and dearest connections, when they stand in competition with the rights of society.

John Adams to Mercy Warren
1776

I have, as yet, met with neither men nor things on this side of the water which abate my predilection, or, if you please, my prejudices, in favor of those on the other. I have but few attachments in Europe much stronger than those we sometimes feel for an accidental fellow-traveller, or for a good inn and a civil landlord. We leave our approbation, and good wishes, and a certain degree of regard with them, by way of paying that part of the reckoning and travelling expenses which money cannot always defray. My affections are deeply rooted in America, and are of too long standing to admit of transplantation. In short, my friend, I can never become so far a citizen of the world as to view every part of it with equal regard; and perhaps nature is wiser in tying our hearts to our native soil, than they are who think they divest themselves of foibles in proportion as they wear away those bonds. It is not difficult to regard men of every nation as members of the same family; but when placed in that point of view, my fellow-citizens appear to me as my brethren, and the others as related to me only in the more distant and adventitious degrees.

John Jay to Gouverneur Morris (from France)
1783

We have been taught here [in the United States] to believe that all power of right belongs to THE PEOPLE— that it flows immediately from them, and is delegated to their officers for the public good—that our rulers are the servants of the people, amenable to their will, and created for their use. How different are the governments of Europe? There the people are the servants and subjects of their rulers. There merit and talents have little or no influence, but all the honors and offices of government are swallowed up by birth, by fortune, or by rank.

From the European world no precedents are to be drawn for a people who think they are capable of governing themselves. Instead of receiving instruction from them, we may with pride assert, that new as this country is in point of settlement; inexperienced as she must be upon questions of government, she still has held forth more useful lessons to the old world—she has made them more acquainted with their own rights, than they had been otherwise for centuries.—It is with pride I repeat, that old and experienced as they are, they are indebted to us for light and refinement upon points of all others the most interesting

Had the American revolution not happened, would Ireland at this time enjoy her present rights of commerce and legislation? Would the subjects of the emperor in the Netherlands have presumed to contend for and ultimately secure the privileges they demanded? Would the parliament of Paris have resisted the edicts of their monarch, and justified this step in a language that would do honor to the freest people? Nay, I may add, would a becoming sense of liberty, and of the rights of mankind, have so generally pervaded that kingdom, had not their knowledge of America led them to the investigation? Undoubtedly not. Let it be therefore our boast, that we have already taught some of the oldest and wisest nations to explore their rights as men; and let it be our prayer, that the effects of our revolution may never cease to operate, until they have unshackled all the nations that have firmness enough to resist the fetters of despotism.

Charles Cotesworth Pinckney
South Carolina Ratifying Convention 1788

When public virtue is gone, when the national spirit is fled . . . the republic is lost in essence, though it may still exist in form.

John Adams to Benjamin Rush
1808

Is it not the glory of the people of America, that whilst they have paid a decent regard to the opinions of former times and other nations, they have not suffered a blind veneration for antiquity, for custom, or for names, to overrule the suggestions of their own good sense, the knowledge of their own situation, and the lessons of their own experience? To this manly spirit, posterity will be indebted for the possession, and the world for the example of the numerous innovations displayed on the American theatre, in favor of private rights and public happiness. Had no important step been taken by the leaders of the revolution for which a precedent could not be discovered, no government established of which an exact model did not present itself, the people of the

United States might, at this moment, have been numbered among the melancholy victims of misguided councils, must at best have been labouring under the weight of some of those forms which have crushed the liberties of the rest of mankind. Happily for America, happily we trust for the whole human race, they pursued a new and more noble course. They accomplished a revolution which has no parallel in the annals of human society: They reared the fabrics of governments which have no model on the face of the globe. They formed the design of a great confederacy, which it is incumbent on their successors to improve and perpetuate. If their works betray imperfections, we wonder at the fewness of them.

James Madison
The Federalist #14 1787

No history now extant can furnish an instance of an army's suffering such uncommon hardships as ours has done and bearing them with the same patience and fortitude. To see men without clothes to cover their nakedness, without blankets to lie on, without shoes (for the want of which their marches might be traced by the blood from their feet) . . . and submitting without a murmur, is a proof of patience and obedience which in my opinion can scarce be paralleled.

George Washington

I am apt to believe that it (the signing of the Declaration of Independence) will be celebrated by succeeding generations, as the great anniversary festival. It ought to be commemorated, as the Day of Deliverance, by solemn acts of devotion to God Almighty. It ought to be solemnized with pomp and parade, with shows, games, sports, guns, bells, bonfires and illuminations, from one end of this continent to the other, from this time forward forevermore.

You will think me transported with enthusiasm, but I am not. I am well aware of the toil and blood and treasure that it will cost to maintain this Declaration, and support and defend these States. Yet through all the gloom I can see the rays of ravishing light and glory. I can see that the end is worth more than all the means, and that posterity will triumph in that day's transactions.

John Adams to Abigail Adams
1776

These are the times that try men's souls; The summer soldier and the sunshine patriot will, in this crisis, shrink from the service of his country; but he that stands it NOW, deserves the love and thanks of man and woman. Tyranny, like hell, is not easily conquered; yet we have this consolation with us, that the harder the conflict, the more glorious the triumph. What we obtain too cheap, we esteem too lightly; "Tis dearness only that gives everything its value. Heaven knows how to put a proper price upon its goods; and it would be strange indeed, if so celestial an article as FREEDOM should not be highly rated.

Thomas Paine
from The Crisis #1

The question now before you (of ratifying the Constitution) is such as no nation on earth, without the limits of America, has ever had the privilege of deciding upon. As the Supreme Ruler of the universe has seen fit to bestow upon us this glorious opportunity, let us decide upon it—appealing to him for the rectitude of our intentions—and in humble confidence that he will yet continue to bless and save our country.

John Hancock
Massachusetts Ratifying Convention 1788

Delightful are the prospects that will open to the view of United America—her sons well prepared to defend their own happiness, and ready to relieve the misery of others—her fleets formidable, but only to the unjust—her revenue sufficient, yet unoppressive—her commerce affluent, without debasing—peace and plenty within her borders—and the glory that arises from a proper use of power, encircling them.

John Dickinson
Letters of Fabius #8 1788

If we wish to be free—if we mean to preserve inviolate those inestimable privileges for which we have been so long contending—if we mean not basely to abandon the noble struggle in which we have been so long engaged, and which we have pledged ourselves never to abandon until the glorious object of our contest shall be obtained—we must fight!—I repeat it, sir, we must fight! An appeal to arms and to the God of Hosts is all that is left us!

They tell us, sir, that we are weak—unable to cope with so formidable an adversary. But when shall we be stronger? Will it be the next week, or the next year? Will it be when we are totally disarmed, and when a British guard shall be stationed in every house? Shall we gather strength by irresolution and inaction? Shall we acquire the means of effectual resistance by lying supinely on our backs, and hugging the delusive phantom of Hope, until our enemies shall have bound us hand and foot? Sir, we are not weak, if we make a proper use of those means which the God of nature hath placed in our power. Three millions of people, armed in the holy cause of liberty, and in such a country as that which we possess, are invincible by any force which our enemy can send against us. Besides, sir, we shall not fight our battles alone. There is a just God who presides over the destinies of nations; and who will raise up friends to fight our battles for us. The battle, sir, is not to the strong alone;

it is to the vigilant, the active, the brave. Besides, sir, we have no election. If we were base enough to desire it, it is now too late to retire from the contest. There is no retreat, but in submission and slavery! Our chains are forged, their clanking may be heard on the plains of Boston! The war is inevitable—and let it come! I repeat it, sir, let it come!

It is vain, sir, to extenuate the matter. Gentlemen may cry, peace, peace—but there is no peace. The war is actually begun! The next gale that sweeps from the north will bring to our ears the clash of resounding arms! Our brethren are already in the field! Why stand we here idle? What is it that gentlemen wish? What would they have? Is life so dear, or peace so sweet, as to be purchased at the price of chains and slavery? Forbid it, Almighty God! I know not what course others may take; but as for me, give me liberty, or give me death!

Patrick Henry
Second Virginia Convention 1775

3

Federal Power

"The powers not delegated to the United States by the Constitution, nor prohibited by it to the states, are reserved to the states respectively, or to the people."

—The Bill of Rights, Article 10

Only in this chapter and two others (Taxes and Term Limits) is it possible to find serious disagreement among the Founders. Although different in specifics, they hinge on the same principle: Big government versus limited government.

The contest which follows is a classic tug-of-war between the advocates of a strong central power and those who tremble at the thought. The rope is the Constitutional phrase, "promote the general welfare" and the chalk-line neatly divides those who view government as MASTER from those who view it as SERVANT, or, as Abraham Lincoln so clearly put it in the Gettysburg Address, "government of the people, by the people, for the people." This is an argument that, in America, is now into its third century. Here you will find no lecture—rather, a lively and powerful debate that pits the great minds of a great age.

Government, like dress, is the badge of lost innocence; the palaces of kings are built on the ruins of the bowers of paradise. For were the impulses of conscience clear, uniform, and irresistibly obeyed, man would need no other lawgiver; but that not being the case, he finds it necessary to surrender up a part of his property to furnish means for the protection of the rest; and this he is induced to do by the same prudence which in every other case advises him out of two evils to choose the least. Wherefore, security being the true design and end of government, it unanswerably follows that whatever form thereof appears most likely to ensure it to us, with the least expense and greatest benefit, is preferable to all others.

Thomas Paine
Common Sense 1776

Nothing is more certain than the indispensable necessity of government, and it is equally undeniable, that whenever and however it is instituted, the people must cede to it some of their natural rights, in order to vest it with requisite powers.

John Jay
The Federalist #2 1788

Government is not reason, it is not eloquence—it is force! Like fire it is a dangerous servant and a fearful master; Never for a moment should it be left to irresponsible action.

George Washington
Farewell Address 1796

In the first place it is to be remembered, that the general government is not to be charged with the whole power of making and administering laws. Its jurisdiction is limited to certain enumerated objects, which concern all the members of the republic, but which are not to be attained by the separate provisions of any. The subordinate governments which can extend their care to all those other objects, which can be separately provided for, will retain their due authority and activity.

James Madison
The Federalist #14 1787

I draw my idea of the form in government from a principle in nature which no art can overturn, viz., that the more simple anything is, the less liable it is to be disordered, and the easier repaired when disordered . . . the constitution of England is so exceedingly complex, that the nation may suffer for years together without being able to discover in which part the fault lies. Some will say in one and some in another, and every political physician will advise a different medicine.

Thomas Paine
Common Sense 1776

A government capable of controlling the whole, and bringing its force to a point, is one of the prerequisites for national liberty . . . if we mean to have our natural rights and properties protected, we must first create a power which is able to do it . . . but power when necessary for our good is as much to be desired as the food we eat or the air we breathe. Some men are mightily afraid of giving power lest it should be improved for oppression; this is doubtless possible, but where is the probability? . . . A power of doing good always implies a power to do evil if the person or party be disposed.

Oliver Ellsworth
A Landholder #3 1787

We all agree that a general government is necessary: But it ought not to go so far as to destroy the authority of the members . . . The state constitutions should be the guardians of our domestic rights and interests; and should be both the support and the check of the federal government.

Melancton Smith
New York Ratifying Convention 1788

The way to have good and safe government is not to trust it all to one, but to divide it among the many, distributing to everyone exactly the functions he is competent to. Let the national government be entrusted to the defense of the nation, and its foreign and federal relations; the state governments with the civil rights, laws, police, and administration of what concerns the state generally; the counties with the local concerns of the counties, and each ward direct the interests within itself. It is by dividing and subdividing these republics from the great national one down through all its subordinations, until it ends in the administration of every man's farm by himself; by placing under everyone what his own eye may superintend, that all will be done for the best. What has destroyed liberty and the rights of man in every government which has ever existed under the sun? The generalizing and concentration of all cares and powers into one body, no matter whether of the autocrats of Russia or France, or of the aristocrats of a Venetian senate.

Thomas Jefferson to Joseph C. Cabell
1816

It is the opinion of the ablest writers on the subject, that no extensive empire can be governed upon republican principles, and that such a government will degenerate to a despotism, unless it be made up of a confederacy of smaller states, each having the full powers of internal regulation. This is precisely the principle which has hitherto preserved our freedom. No instance can be found of any free government of considerable extent which has been supported upon any other plan. Large and consolidated empires may indeed dazzle the eyes of a distant spectator with their splendour, but if examined more nearly are always found to be full of misery. The reason is obvious. In large states the same principles of legislation will not apply to all the parts . . . We accordingly find that the very great empires have always been despotic. They have indeed tried to remedy the inconveniences to which the people were exposed by local regulation; but these contrivances have never answered the end. The laws not being made by the people, who felt the inconveniences, did not suit their circumstances. It is under such tyranny that the Spanish provinces languish, and such would be our misfortune and degradation, if we should submit to have the concerns of the whole empire managed by one legislature. To promote the happiness of the people it is necessary that there should be local laws; and it is necessary that those laws should be made by the representatives of those who are immediately subject to the want of them. By endeavouring to suit both extremes, both are injured.

James Winthrop
Massachusetts Ratifying Convention 1787

The gentleman last on the floor, has informed us, that according to his idea of a complete representation, the extent of our country is too great for it . . . I take it [however], that no federal government is worth having, unless it can provide for the general interests of the United States.

John Jay
New York Ratifying Convention 1788

This, at all events, must be evident, that the very difficulty itself, drawn from the extent of the country, is the strongest argument in favor of an energetic government; for any other can certainly never preserve the Union of so large an empire.

Alexander Hamilton
The Federalist #23 1788

...when once an efficient national government is established, the best men in the country will not only consent to serve, but also will generally be appointed to manage it; for, although town or country, or other contracted influence, may place men in State assemblies, or senates, or courts of justice, or executive departments, yet more general and extensive reputation for talents and other qualifications will be necessary to recommend men to offices under the national government—especially as it will have the widest field for choice, and never experience that want of proper persons which is not uncommon in some of the states. Hence, it will result that the administration, the political counsels, and the judicial decisions of the national government will be more wise, systematical, and judicious than those of individual states, and consequently more satisfactory with respect to other nations, as well as more safe with respect to us.

John Jay
The Federalist #3 1788

The Constitution defines the powers of Congress; and every power not expressly delegated to that body, remains in the several state-legislatures. The sovereignty and the republican form of government of each state is guaranteed by the constitution; and the bounds of jurisdiction between the federal and respective state governments, are marked with precision.

Noah Webster
1787

Temporary deviations from fundamental principles are always more or less dangerous. When the first pretext fails, those who become interested in prolonging the evil will rarely be at a loss for other pretexts.

James Madison
1785

It is true that impositions for raising a revenue may be hereafter called regulations of trade; but names will not change the nature of things. Indeed we ought firmly to believe, what is an undoubted truth, confirmed by the unhappy experience of many states heretofore free, that UNLESS THE MOST WATCHFUL ATTENTION BE EXERTED, A NEW SERVITUDE MAY BE SLIPPED UPON US, UNDER THE SANCTION OF USUAL AND RESPECTABLE TERMS.

Thus the Caesars ruined the Roman liberty, under the titles of tribunical and dictatorial authorities, old and venerable dignities, known in the most flourishing times of freedom. In imitation of the same policy, James II, when he meant to establish popery, talked of liberty of conscience, the most sacred of all liberties; and had thereby almost deceived the dissenters into destruction.

All artful rulers, who strive to extend their power beyond its just limits, endeavor to give to their attempts as much semblance of legality as possible. Those who succeed them may venture to go a little further; for each new encroachment will be strengthened by a former. "That which is now supported by examples, growing old, will become an example itself," (Tacitus) and thus support fresh usurpations. A free people therefore can never be too quick in observing, nor too firm in opposing the beginnings of alteration either in form or reality, respecting institutions formed for their security. The first kind of alteration leads to the last: Yet, on the other hand, nothing is more certain, than that the forms of liberty may be retained, when the substance is gone.

John Dickinson
Letters from a Farmer in Pennsylvania #5 1768

As the cool and deliberate sense of the community ought, in all governments, and actually will, in all free governments, ultimately prevail over the views of its rulers; so there are particular moments in public affairs when the people, stimulated by some irregular passion, or some illicit advantage, or misled by the artful misrepresentations of interested men, may call for measures which they themselves will afterwards be the most ready to lament and condemn. In these critical moments, how salutary will be the interference of some temperate and respectable body of citizens, in order to check the misguided career, and to suspend the blow meditated by the people against themselves, until reason, justice, and truth can regain their authority over the public mind?

Alexander Hamilton or James Madison
The Federalist #63 1788

I believe the great body of our people to be virtuous and friendly to good government, to the protection of liberty and property; and it is the duty of all good men, especially of those who are placed as sentinels to guard their rights—it is their duty to examine into the prevailing politics of parties, and to disclose them—while they avoid exciting undue suspicions, to lay facts before the people, which will enable them to form a proper judgment. Men who wish the people of the country to determine for themselves, and deliberately to fit the government to their situation, must feel some degree of indignation at those attempts to hurry the adoption of a system, and to shut the door against examination. The very attempts create suspicions, that those who make them have secret views, or see some defects in the system, which, in the hurry of affairs, they expect will escape the eye of a free people . . .

It is natural for men, who wish to hasten the adoption of a measure, to tell us, now is the crisis—now is the critical moment which must be seized or all will be lost; and to shut the door against free enquiry, whenever conscious the thing presented has defects in it, which time and investigation will probably discover. This has been the custom of tyrants, and their dependents in all ages.

Richard Henry Lee
Letters from the Federal Farmer #5,#1 1787

It is unfair to presume that the representatives of the people will be disposed to tyrannize in one government more than in another. If we are convinced that the national legislature will pursue a system of measures unfavorable to the interests of the people, we ought to have no general government at all. But if we unite, it will be for the accomplishment of great purposes: These demand great resources, and great powers.

Alexander Hamilton
New York Ratifying Convention 1788

When we consider that this government is charged with the external and mutual relations only of these states; that the states themselves have principal care of our persons, our property, and our reputation, constituting the great field of human concerns, we may well doubt whether our organization is not too complicated, too expensive; whether offices or officers have not been multiplied unnecessarily, and sometimes injuriously to the service they were meant to promote. I will cause to be laid before you an essay toward a statement of those who, under public employment of various kinds, draw money from the treasury or from our citizens. The inspectors of internal revenue who were found to obstruct the accountability of the institution have been discontinued. Several agencies created by executive authority, on salaries fixed by that also, have been suppressed.

Thomas Jefferson
First Annual Message 1801

Every view we may take of the subject, as candid inquirers after the truth, will serve to convince us, that it is both unwise and dangerous to deny the federal government an unconfined authority, as to all those objects which are intrusted to its management . . . The POWERS are not too extensive for the OBJECTS of federal administration, or, in other words, for the management of our NATIONAL INTERESTS; nor can any satisfactory argument be framed to show that they are chargeable with such an excess.

Alexander Hamilton
The Federalist #23 1788

There are certain inalienable and fundamental rights, which in forming the social compact, ought to be explicitly ascertained and fixed—a free and enlightened people, in forming this compact, will not resign all their rights to those who govern, and they will fix limits to their legislators and rulers, which will soon be plainly seen by those who are governed, as well as by those who govern: and the latter will know they cannot be passed unperceived by the former, and without giving a general alarm.

Richard Henry Lee
Letters of a Federal Farmer #2 1787

WHO ARE THE BEST KEEPERS OF THE PEOPLE'S LIBERTIES?

Republican—The people themselves. The sacred trust can be nowhere safe as in the hands most interested in preserving it.

Anti-republican—The people are stupid, suspicious, licentious. They cannot safely trust themselves. When they have established government they should think of nothing but obedience, leaving the care of their liberties to their wiser rulers.

Republican—Although all men are born free, and all nations might be so, yet too true it is, that slavery has been the general lot of the human race. Ignorant—they have been cheated; asleep—they have been surprised; divided—the yoke has been forced upon them. But what is the lesson? That because the people may betray themselves, they ought to give themselves up, blindfold, to those who have an interest in betraying them? Rather conclude that the people ought to be enlightened, to be awakened, to be united, that after establishing a government they should watch over it, as well as obey it.

Anti-republican—You look at the surface only, where errors float, instead of fathoming the depths where truth lies hid. It is not the government that is disposed to fly off from the people; but the people that are ever ready to fly off from the government. Rather say then, enlighten the government, warn it to be vigilant, enrich it with influence, arm it with force, and to the people never pronounce but two words—Submission and Confidence.

Republican—The centrifugal tendency then is in the people, not in the government, and the secret art lies in restraining the tendency, by augmenting the attractive principle of the government with all the weight that can be added to it. What a perversion of the natural order of things! To make power the primary and central object of the social system, and Liberty but its satellite.

Anti-republican—The science of the stars can never instruct you in the mysteries of government. Wonderful as it may seem, the more you increase the attractive force of power, the more you enlarge the sphere of liberty. The more you make government independent and hostile towards the people, the better security you provide for their rights and interests...

Republican—But mysteries belong to religion, not to government; to the ways of the Almighty, not to the works of man. And in religion itself there is nothing mysterious to its author; the mystery lies in the dimness of the human sight. So in the institutions of man let there by no mystery . . .

Anti-republican—You are destitute, I perceive, of every quality of a good citizen, or rather of a good subject. You have neither the light of faith nor the spirit of obedience. I denounce you to the government as an accomplice of atheism and anarchy.

Republican—And I forbear to denounce you to the people, though a blasphemer of their rights and an idolater of tyranny. Liberty disdains to persecute.

James Madison
1792

An enlightened zeal for the energy and efficiency of government will be stigmatized as the offspring of a temper fond of despotic power and hostile to the principles of liberty . . .
It will be forgotten, on the one hand, that jealousy is the usual concomitant of love, and that the noble enthusiasm of liberty is apt to be infected with a spirit of narrow and illiberal distrust. On the other hand, it will be equally forgotten that the vigor of government is essential to the security of liberty . . . and that a dangerous ambition more often lurks behind the specious mask of zeal for the rights of the people than under the forbidding appearance of zeal for the firmness and efficiency of government.

Alexander Hamilton
The Federalist #1 1788

When an act injurious to freedom has been once done, and the people bear it, the repetition of it is most likely to meet with submission. For as the mischief of the one was found to be tolerable, they will hope that of the second will prove so too; and they will not regard the infamy of the last, because they are stained with that of the first.
Indeed nations, in general, are not apt to think until they feel; and therefore nations in general have lost

their liberty: For as violations of the rights of the governed are commonly not only specious, but small at the beginning, they spread over the multitude in such a manner, as to touch individuals but slightly. Thus they are disregarded. The power or profit that arises from these violations, centering in few persons, is to them considerable. For this reason the governors having in view their particular purposes, successively preserve a uniformity of conduct for attaining them. They regularly increase the first injuries, till at length the inattentive people are compelled to perceive the heaviness of their burdens.—They begin to complain and inquire—but too late. They find their oppressors so strengthened by success, and themselves so entangled in examples of express authority on the part of their rulers, and tacit recognition on their own part, that they are quite confounded; For millions entertain no other idea of the legality of power, than that it is founded on the exercise of power. They voluntarily fasten their chains, by adopting a pusillanimous opinion, "that there will be too much danger in attempting a remedy,"—or another opinion no less fatal,—"that the government has a right to treat them as it does." They then seek a wretched relief for their minds, by persuading themselves, that to yield their obedience is to discharge their duty. The deplorable poverty of spirit, that prostrates all the dignity bestowed by Divine Providence on our nature—of course succeeds.

From these reflections I conclude, that every free state should incessantly watch, and instantly take alarm on any addition being made to the power exercised over them. Innumerable instances might be produced to show, from what slight beginnings the most extensive consequences have flowed: But I shall select two only from the history of England.

Henry the Seventh was the first monarch of that kingdom, who established A STANDING BODY OF ARMED MEN. This was a band of fifty archers, called yeomen of the guard: And this institution, notwithstanding the smallness of the number, was, to prevent discontent, "disguised under pretence of majesty and grandeur." In 1684 the standing forces were so much augmented, that Rapin says—"The king, in order to make his people fully sensible of their new slavery, affected to muster his troops, which amounted to 4000 well armed and disciplined men." I think our army, at this time, consists of more than seventy regiments.

The method of taxing by EXCISE was first introduced amidst the convulsions of civil wars. Extreme necessity was pretended for it, and its short continuance promised. After the restoration, and excise upon beer, ale and other liquors, was granted to the king, one half in fee, the other for life, as an equivalent for the court of wards. Upon James the Second's accession, the parliament gave him the first excise, with an additional duty on wine, tobacco, and some other things. Since the revolution it has been extended to salt, candles, leather, hides, hops, soap, paper, paste-boards, mill-boards, scale-boards, vellum, parchment, starch, silks, calicoes, linens, stuffs, printed, stained, and etc. wire, wrought plate, coffee, tea, chocolate, and etc.

Thus a standing army and excise have, from their first slender origins, though always hated, always feared, always opposed, at length swelled up to their vast present bulk.

These facts are sufficient to support what I have said. 'Tis true, that all the mischiefs apprehended by our ancestors from a standing army and excise, have not yet happened: But it does not follow from thence that they will not happen. The inside of a house may catch fire, and most valuable apartments be ruined, before the flames burst out. The question in these cases is not, what evil has actually attended particular measures— but, what evil, in the nature of things, is likely to attend them.

John Dickinson
Letters from a Farmer in Pennsylvania #11 1768

It is an observation of an eminent patriot, that a people long inured to hardships, loose by degrees the very notions of liberty; they look upon themselves as creatures at mercy, and that all impositions laid on by superior hands, are legal and obligatory. But thank Heaven this is not yet verified in America! We have yet some share of public virtue remaining.

Samuel Adams
1772

Our country is too large to have all its affairs directed by a single government. Public servants, at such a distance, and from under the eye of their constituents, must, from the circumstance of distance, be unable to administer and overlook all the details necessary for the good government of the citizens; and the same circumstance, by rendering detection impossible to their constituents, will invite the public agents to corruption, plunder, and waste. And I do truly believe that if the principle were to prevail in the United States in which the general government possesses all the powers of the state governments, and reduces us to a single consolidated government, it would become the most corrupt government on the earth. You have seen the practices by which the public servants have been able to cover their conduct, or, where that could not be done, delusions by which they have varnished it for the eye of their constituents. What an augmentation of the field for jobbing, speculating, plundering, office building, and office hunting would be produced by an assumption of all the state powers into the hands of the general government!

Thomas Jefferson
Second Inaugural Address 1805

But it is said that the laws of the Union are to be the supreme law of the land. But what inference can be drawn from this, or what would they amount to, if they were not to be supreme? It is evident they would amount to nothing. A LAW, by the very meaning of the term, includes supremacy. It is a rule which those to whom it is prescribed are bound to observe . . . If a number of political societies enter into a larger political society, the laws which the latter may enact, pursuant to the powers intrusted to it by its constitution, must necessarily be supreme over those societies, and the individuals of whom they are composed. It would otherwise be a mere treaty, dependent on the good faith of the parties, and not a government, which is only another word for POLITI-CAL POWER AND SUPREMACY.

Alexander Hamilton
The Federalist #33 1788

Our duty is to frame a government friendly to lib-erty and the rights of mankind, which will tend to cher-ish and cultivate a love of liberty among our citizens. If this government becomes oppressive it will be by de-grees: It will aim at its end by disseminating sentiments of government opposite to republicanism; and proceed from step to step in depriving the people of a share in the government.

Melancton Smith
New York Ratifying Convention 1788

A good administration will conciliate the confidence and affectation of the people and perhaps enable the government to acquire more consistency than the pro-posed constitution seems to promise for so great a Coun-try—It may then triumph altogether over the state gov-ernments and reduce them to an entire subordination, dividing the large states into smaller districts. The or-gans of the general government may also acquire addi-tional strength.

If this should not be the case, in the course of a few years, it is probable that the contests about the boundaries of power between the particular governments and the general government and the momentum of the larger states in such contests will produce a dissolution of the Union. This after all seems to be the most likely result.

Alexander Hamilton
1787

The powers delegated by the proposed Constitution to the federal government, are few and defined. Those which are to remain in the state governments are numerous and indefinite. The former will be exercised principally on external objects, as war, peace, negotiation, and foreign commerce; with which last the power of taxation will for the most part be connected. The powers reserved to the several states will extend to all the objects, which, in the ordinary course of affairs, concern the lives, liberties and properties of the people; and the internal order, improvement, and prosperity of the state.

The operations of the federal government will be most extensive and important in times of war and danger; those of the state governments, in times of peace and security. As the former periods will probably bear a small proportion to the latter, the state governments will here enjoy another advantage over the federal government. The more adequate indeed the federal powers may be rendered to the national defense, the less frequent will be those scenes of danger which might favor their ascendancy over the governments of the particular states.

James Madison
The Federalist #45 1788

I lament with you the political disorders England at present labours under . . . In my humble opinion, the root of the evil lies not so much in too long, or too unequally chosen Parliaments, as in the enormous salaries, emoluments, and patronage of your great offices; and that you will never be at rest till they are all abolished, and every place of honour made at the same time, instead of a place of profit, a place of expense and burden.

Benjamin Franklin to William Strahan
1784

Some boast of being friends to government; I am a friend to righteous government founded upon the principles of reason and justice; but I glory in publicly avowing my eternal enmity to tyranny.

John Hancock
1774

How easy it is to persuade men to sign anything by which they can't be affected!

George Mason to Zachariah Johnston
1791

Few men are contented with less power than they have a right to exercise.

Samuel Adams to Richard Henry Lee
1789

4

Crime

"... establish justice,
insure domestic tranquility ..."

—The U.S. Constitution

---

*Perhaps this chapter would be more aptly titled "Justice,"
for this is the simple answer the founders gave to the problem
of crime. They, like wise King Solomon, knew that, "Because
sentence against an evil work is not executed speedily, therefore
the heart of men is fully set in them to do evil."*

*In the following few pages, we find men laying down
feelings, very strong at times, in order to carry out good sense.
Justice without mercy will destroy a man, but mercy without
justice will destroy mankind. Ultimately, good sense, not good
feelings, WILL be mercy—to society at large. For justice makes
a bad man fear, and fear makes him change. Inversely, lenity
robs him of his fear and, in so doing, adds to those of society's.*

"Punishment is a sort of medicine."

—*Aristotle*

It frequently happens that wicked and dissolute men, resigning themselves to the dominion of inordinate passions, commit violations on the lives, liberties, and properties of others, and the secure enjoyment of these having principally induced men to enter into society, government would be defective in its principle purpose, were it not to restrain such criminal acts by inflicting due punishments on those who perpetrate them; but it appears at the same time equally deducible from the purposes of society, that a member thereof, committing an inferior injury, does not wholly forfeit the protection of his fellow citizens, but after suffering a punishment in proportion to his offense, is entitled to their protection from all greater pain, so that it becomes a duty in the legislature to arrange in a proper scale the crimes which it may be necessary for them to repress, and to adjust thereto a corresponding gradation of punishments:

• If a husband murder his wife, a parent his child, or a child his parent, he shall suffer death by hanging.

• Whoever shall commit murder by poisoning, shall suffer death by poison.

• Whoever shall commit murder in any other way shall suffer death by hanging.

• Whoever shall be guilty of manslaughter shall for the first offense, be condemned to hard labor for seven years in the public works; shall forfeit one half of his lands and goods to the next of kin to the person slain, the other half to be sequestered during such term, in the hands, and to the use, of the commonwealth, allowing a reasonable part of the profits for the support of his family. The second offense shall be deemed murder.

• Whenever sentence of death shall have been pronounced against any person for treason or murder, execution thereof shall be done the next day but one after such sentence, unless it be Sunday, and then on the Monday following.

5555

• (Whatever man) shall be guilty of rape, polygamy, or sodomy shall be punished by castration.

• Whoever on purpose shall disfigure another . . . shall be maimed or disfigured in like sort . . . and moreover shall forfeit one half of his lands and goods to the sufferer.

• Whoever commits arson shall be condemned to hard labor in the public works and shall make good the loss of the sufferers threefold.

• Whoever commits robbery shall be condemned to hard labor four years in the public works and shall make double reparations to the person injured.

Thomas Jefferson
from a bill for Proportioning
Crimes and Punishments

The Administration of justice is the firmest pillar of government.

George Washington to Edmund Randolph
1789

The business of civil government is to protect the citizen in his rights, to defend the community from hostile powers, and to promote the general welfare. Civil government has no business to meddle with the private opinions of the people. If I demean myself as a good citizen, I am accountable, not to man, but to God, for the religious opinions which I embrace, and the manner in which I worship the supreme being . . . But while I assert the right of religious liberty; I would not deny that the civil power has a right, in some cases, to interfere in matters of religion. It has a right to prohibit and punish gross immoralities and impieties; because the open practice of these is of evil example and public detriment. For this reason, I heartily approve of our laws against drunkenness, profane swearing, blasphemy, and professed atheism.

Oliver Ellsworth
Connecticut Ratifying Convention 1787

I always hear of capital executions with concern, and regret that there should occur so many instances in which they are necessary.

George Washington to General Clinton
1778

I am now engaged in the most disagreeable part of my duty, trying criminals... Punishment must of course become certain, and mercy dormant—a harsh system, repugnant to my feelings, but nevertheless necessary.

John Jay
1778

The execution of the laws is more important than the making them.

Thomas Jefferson to Abbe' Arnond
1789

Penitence must precede pardon.

John Adams
The Sedition Act 1798

It would have been a truth, if Mr. Locke had not said it, that where there is no law, there can be no liberty, and nothing deserves the name of law but that which is certain and universal in its operation upon all the members of the community.

To look up to a government that establishes justice, insures order, cherishes virtue, secures property, and protects from every species of violence, affords a pleasure that can only be exceeded by looking up in all circumstances to an overruling providence.—Such a pleasure I hope is before us, and our posterity under the influence of the new government.

Benjamin Rush to David Ramsay
1788

No punishment in my opinion is too great for the man who can build his greatness upon his Country's ruin.

George Washington
1778

5

Taxes

*" . . . We have warned them
from time to time of attempts by their
legislature to extend an unwarrantable
jurisdiction over us . . ."*

—The Declaration of Independence

———————

"The power to tax is the power to destroy," warned our *30th President, Calvin Coolidge, ". . . a government which lays taxes on the people not required by urgent public necessity and sound public policy is not a protector of liberty, but an instrument of tyranny."*

One of the simplest arguments against high taxes is this: The government requires an inordinate amount of income because it is exercising a plethora of unconstitutional functions which are neither urgent necessity nor sound policy. In a word, it is offering its citizens security in exchange for freedom. Those taxes remain wonderfully affordable which are paid to a sound and equitable government; one dedicated to the principles of personal responsibility and self-reliance. These are the twin-tools which forge an individual's, and a nation's, freedom.

———————

Sir, there are two passions which have a powerful influence in the affairs of men. These are ambition and avarice: The love of power and the love of money. Separately, each of these has a great force in prompting men to action, but when united in view of the same object, they have in many minds the most violent of effects. Place before the minds of such men a post of honor that shall at the same time be a place of profit, and they will move heaven and earth to obtain it. The vast number of such places it is that renders the British government so tempestuous . . . besides these evils, sir, though we may set out in the beginning with moderate salaries, we shall find that such will not be of long continuance. Reasons will never be wanting for proposed augmentations; and there will always be a party for giving more to the rulers, that the rulers may be able in return to give more to them. Hence, as all history informs us, there has been in every state and kingdom a constant kind of warfare between the governing and the governed; the one striving to obtain more for its support, and the other to pay less.

Benjamin Franklin
From speech at the Constitutional Convention 1787

It is not the judgement of free people only, that money for defending them, is safest in their own keeping, but it has also been the opinion of the best and wisest kings and governors of mankind, in every age of the world, that the wealth of a state was most securely as well as most profitably deposited in the hands of their faithful subjects. Constantius, emperor of the Romans, though an absolute prince, both practiced and praised this method.

Stephen Hopkins
The Rights of Colonies Examined 1764

However extensive the constitutional power of a government to impose taxes may be, I think it should not be so exercised as to impede or discourage the lawful and useful industry and exertions of individuals. Hence, the prudence of taxing the products of beneficial labor, either mental or manual, appears to be at least questionable . . . Whether taxation should extend only to property, or only to income, are points on which opinions have not been uniform. I am inclined to think that both should not be taxed.

John Jay
1812

As to poll taxes, I, without scruple, confess my disapprobation of them, and . . . I should lament to see them introduced into practice under the national government. But does it follow because there is a power to lay them, that they will actually be laid? . . . As little friendly as I am to (that) species of imposition, I still feel a thorough conviction, that the power of having recourse to it ought to exist in the federal government. There are certain emergencies of nations, in which expedients that in the ordinary state of things ought to be forborne, become essential to the public well-being. And the government from the possibility of such emergencies ought ever to have the option of making use of them.

Alexander Hamilton
The Federalist #36 1788

Spain was once free. Their Cortes resembled our parliaments. No money could be raised on the subjects, without their consent. One of their kings having received a grant from them, to maintain a war against the Moors, desired, that if the sum which they had given, should not be sufficient, he might be allowed, for that emergency only, to raise more money without assembling the Cortes. The request was violently opposed by

the best and wisest men in the assembly. It was, however, complied with by the votes of a majority; and this
single concession was a PRECEDENT for other conces-
sions of the like kind, until at last the crown obtained a
general power of raising money, in cases of necessity.
From that period the Cortes ceased to be useful—the
people ceased to be free.

Venienti occurite morbo.
Oppose a disease at its beginning.

John Dickinson
Letters from A Pennsylvania Farmer

It is a general maxim, that all governments find a
use for as much money as they can raise. Indeed they
have commonly demands for more: Hence it is, that all,
as far as we are acquainted, are in debt. I take this to be
a settled truth, that they will spend as much as their
revenue; that is, will live at least up to their income.
Congress will ever exercise their powers, to levy as much
money as the people can pay. They will not be restrained
from direct taxes, by the consideration that necessity
does not require them. If they forbear, it will be because
the people cannot answer their demands.

Melancton Smith
New York Ratifying Convention 1788

At home, fellow citizens, you best know whether we
have done well or ill. The suppression of unnecessary
offices, of useless establishments and expenses, enabled
us to discontinue our internal taxes. These covering our
land with officers, and opening our doors to their intru-
sions, had already begun that process of domiciliary vexa-
tion which, once entered, is scarcely to be restrained
from reaching successively every article of produce and
property.

Thomas Jefferson
Second Inaugural Address 1805

It is a signal advantage of taxes on articles of consumption (sales tax), that they contain in their own nature a security against excess. They prescribe their own limit; which cannot be exceeded without defeating the end proposed—that is an extension of the revenue. When applied to this object, the saying is as just as it is witty, that "in political arithmetic, two and two do not always make four." If duties are too high they lessen the consumption—the collection is eluded; and the product to the treasury is not so great as when they are confined within proper and moderate bounds. This forms a complete barrier against any material oppression of the citizens, by taxes of this class, and is itself a natural limitation of the power of imposing them.

Impositions of this kind usually fall under the denomination of indirect taxes, and must always constitute the chief part of the revenue raised in this country.

Alexander Hamilton
The Federalist #21 1787

Direct taxation can go but little way towards raising a revenue. To raise money in this way, people must be provident; they must be constantly laying up money to answer the demands of the collector. But you cannot make people thus provident; if you would do anything to purpose you must come in when they are spending, and take a part with them. This does not take away the tools of a man's business, or the necessary utensils of his family: It only comes in when he is taking his pleasure, and feels generous . . .

Oliver Ellsworth
Connecticut Ratifying Convention 1788

When a certain sum comes to be taxed, and the mode of levying to be fixed, (Congress) will lay the tax on that article which will be most productive, and easiest in the collection, without consulting the real circumstances or convenience of a state, with which, in fact, they cannot be sufficiently acquainted. The mode of levying taxes is of the utmost consequence, and yet here it is to be determined by those who have neither knowledge of our situation, nor a common interest with us, nor a fellow feeling for us: the subjects of taxation differ in three-fourths; nay, I might say with truth, in four-fifths of the states: if we trust the national government with an effectual way of raising the necessary sums, 'tis sufficient; everything we do further is trusting the happiness and rights of the people: why then should we give up this dangerous power of individual taxation? Why leave the manner of laying taxes to those, who in the nature of things, cannot be acquainted with the situation of those on whom they are to impose them, when it can be done by those who are well acquainted with it? If instead of giving this oppressive power, we give them such an effectual alternative as will answer the purpose, without encountering the evil and danger that might arise from it, then I would cheerfully acquiesce . . . If we give the general government the power of demanding their quotas of the states, with an alternative of laying direct taxes, in case of non compliance, then the mischief would be avoided; and the certainty of this conditional power would, in all human probability, prevent the application, and the sums necessary for the union would be then laid by the states, by those who know how it can best be raised, by those who have a fellow-feeling for us.

George Mason
Virginia Ratifying Convention 1788

It has been asserted that a power of internal taxation in the national legislature could never be exercised with advantage, as well from the want of a sufficient knowledge of local circumstances as from an interference between the revenue laws of the Union and of the particular states. The supposition of a want of proper knowledge, seems to be entirely destitute of foundation. If any question is depending in a state legislature respecting one of the counties which demands a knowledge of local details, how is it acquired? No doubt from the information of the members of the county. Cannot the like knowledge be obtained in the national legislature from the representatives of each state? And is it not to be presumed that the men who will generally be sent there, will be possessed of the necessary degree of intelligence, to be able to communicate that information?

Alexander Hamilton
The Federalist #36 1788

There are two ways of laying taxes. One is, by imposing a certain sum on particular kinds of property, to be paid by the user or consumer, or by rating the person at a certain sum. The other is, by imposing a certain sum on particular kinds of property, to be paid by the seller.

When a man pays the first sort of tax, he knows with certainty that he pays so much money for a tax. The consideration for which he pays it, is remote, and, it may be, does not occur to him. He is sensible too, that he is commanded and obliged to pay it as a tax; and therefore people are apt to be displeased with this sort of tax.

The other sort of tax is submitted to in a very different manner. The purchaser of an article, very seldom reflects that the seller raises his price, so as to indemnify himself for the tax he has paid. He knows that the prices of things are continually fluctuating, and if he thinks about the tax, he thinks at the same time, in all probability, that he might have paid as much, if the article he buys had not been taxed. He gets something visible and agreeable for his money; and tax and price are so confounded together, that he cannot separate, or does not choose to take the trouble of separating them.

This mode of taxation therefore is the mode suited to arbitrary and oppressive governments. The love of liberty is so natural to the human heart, that unfeeling tyrants think themselves obliged to accommodate their schemes as much as they can to the appearance of justice and reason, and to deceive those whom they resolve to destroy, or oppress, by presenting to them a miserable picture of freedom, when the inestimable original is lost.

This policy did not escape the cruel and rapacious NERO. That monster, apprehensive that his crimes might endanger his authority and life, thought proper to do some popular acts, to secure the obedience of his subjects. Among other things, says Tacitus, "he remitted the twenty-fifth part of the price on the sale of slaves, but rather in show than in reality; for the seller being ordered to pay it, it became part of the price to the buyer."

This is the reflection of the judicious Historian; but the deluded people gave their infamous Emperor full credit for his false generosity. Other nations have been treated in the same manner the Romans were. The honest, industrious Germans, who are settled in different parts of this continent, can inform us, that it was this sort of tax that drove them from their native land to our woods, at that time the seats of perfect and undisturbed freedom.

Their Princes, inflamed by the lust of power, and the lust of avarice, two furies that the more they are gorged, the more hungry they grow, transgressed the bounds they ought, in regard to themselves, to have observed.

John Dickinson
Letters from a Pennsylvania Farmer

We must make our election between economy and liberty, or profusion and servitude. If we run into such debts as that we must be taxed in our meat and in our drink, in our necessaries and our comforts, in our labors and our amusements, for our callings and our creeds, as the people of England are, our people, like them, must come to labor sixteen hours in the twenty-four, give the earnings of fifteen of these to the government for their debts and daily expenses; and the sixteenth being insufficient to afford us bread, we must live, as they now do, on oatmeal and potatoes; have no time to think, no means of calling the mismanagers to account; but be glad to obtain subsistence by hiring ourselves to rivet their chains on the necks of our fellow-sufferers . . . This example reads to us the salutary lesson, that private fortunes are destroyed by public as well as by private extravagance. And this is the tendency of all human governments. A departure from principle in one instance becomes a precedent for a second; that second for a third; and so on, till the bulk of the society is reduced to be mere automatons of misery, and to have no sensibilities left but for sinning and suffering.

Thomas Jefferson to Samuel Kercheval
1816

I sincerely believe . . . that the principle of spending money to be paid by posterity, under the name of funding, is but swindling futurity on a large scale.

Thomas Jefferson to John Taylor
1816

How to make a STRIKING SUNDIAL, by which not only a man's own family, but all his neighbours for ten miles round, may know what o'clock it is, when the sun shines, without seeing the dial:

Choose an open place in your yard or garden, on which the sun may shine all day without any impediment from trees or buildings. On the ground mark out your hour lines, as for a horizontal dial, according to art, taking room enough for the guns. On the line for one o'clock, place one gun; on the two o'clock line two guns, and so of the rest. The guns must all be charged with powder, but ball is unnecessary. Your gnomon or style must have twelve magnifying glasses annexed to it, and be so placed as that the sun shining through the glasses, one after the other, shall cause the focus or burning spot to fall on the hour line of one, for example, at one o'clock, and there kindle a train of gunpowder that shall fire one gun. At two o'clock, a focus shall fall on the hour line of two, and kindle another train that shall discharge two guns successively; and so of the rest.

Note, there must be 78 guns in all. Thirty-two pounders will be best for this use; but 18 pounders may do, and will cost less, as well as use less powder, for nine pounds of powder will do for one charge of each eighteen pounder, whereas the thirty-two pounders would require for each gun 16 pounds.

Note also, that the chief expense will be the powder, for the cannon once bought, will, with care, last 100 years.

Note moreover, that there will be a great saving of powder on cloudy days.

Kind reader, Methinks I hear thee say, That it is indeed a good thing to know how the time passes, but this kind of dial, notwithstanding the mentioned savings, would be very expensive; and the cost greater than the advantage. Thou art wise, my friend, to be so thoughtful beforehand; some fools would not have found out so much, till they had made the dial and try'd it.—Let all such learn that many a private and many a public project, are like this Striking Dial, great cost for little profit.

Benjamin Franklin
Poor Richard Improved 1757

6

Education

"... promote the general welfare, and secure the blessings of liberty to ourselves and our posterity ..."

—Pre Amble to the
U.S. Constitution

Of all the influences which helped to shape the thinking of the founding fathers and their framing of the new republic, perhaps none was greater than that of renowned English philosopher John Locke. His idea of "inalienable rights" was the very heart of the Declaration of Independence, and continues to be the cornerstone of the American experience. Ben Franklin's article at the end of this chapter contains the following from Locke: " 'Tis VIRTUE, then, direct VIRTUE which is to be aimed at in education. All other considerations and accomplishments are nothing in comparison to this." The question then arises why any and all mention in the schools of "direct virtue" has been exterminated on the grounds that an individual's "inalienable rights" may be infringed. This is demented logic (the result of which is criminal). For it is virtue alone that can guarantee a society the preservation of its "inalienable rights." A piece of paper just will not do it—even if it is called the Bill of Rights. Maybe this is what John Adams meant when he said, "The only foundation of a free constitution is pure virtue."

If a nation expects to be ignorant and free in a state of civilization, it expects what never was and never will be.

Thomas Jefferson to Colonel Charles Yancey
1816

A diffusion of knowledge is the only guardian of true liberty.

James Madison to George Thompson
1825

Every child in America should be acquainted with his own country. He should read books that furnish him with ideas that will be useful to him in life and practice. As soon as he opens his lips, he should rehearse the history of his own country; he should lisp the praise of liberty and of those illustrious heroes and statesmen who have wrought a revolution in her favor.

A selection of essays respecting the settlement and geography of America, the history of the late Revolution and of the most remarkable characters and events that distinguished it, and a compendium of the principles of the federal and provincial governments should be the principal schoolbook in the United States. These are interesting objects to every man; they call home the minds of youth and fix them upon the interests of their own country, and they assist in forming attachments to it, as well as in enlarging the understanding . . .

Two regulations are essential to the continuance of republican governments; (1) Such a distribution of lands and such principles of descent and alienation as shall give every citizen a power of acquiring what his industry merits. (2) Such a system of education as gives every citizen an opportunity of acquiring knowledge and fitting himself for places of trust. These are fundamental articles, the sine qua non of the existence of the American republics . . .

... children should be taught the usual branches of learning, submission to superiors and to laws, the moral or social duties, the history and transactions of their own country, the principles of liberty and government ... The virtues of men are of more consequence to society than their abilities, and for this reason the heart should be cultivated with more assiduity than the head. Are parents and guardians ignorant that children always imitate those with whom they live or associate? .... It is therefore a point of infinite importance to society that youth should not associate with persons whose manners they ought not to imitate ... For these reasons children should keep the best of company that they might have before them the best manners, the best upbringing, and the best conversation. Their minds should be kept untainted till their reasoning faculties have acquired strength and the good principles which may be planted in their minds have taken deep root. They will then be able to make a firm and probably a successful resistance against the attacks of secret corruption and brazen libertinism.

Noah Webster
1790

I observe in your letter the strongest inclination for obtaining a large fund of useful knowledge to be drawn from reading history. If we act only for ourselves, to neglect the study of history is not prudent. If we are entrusted with the cares of others it is not just. Ignorance when it is voluntary is criminal, and he may be properly charged with evil who refuses to learn how he might prevent it ... Think not, my dear friend, because I caution you against evil I think you already vicious. Before habits are established, friendships confirmed, and life planned into method, the infant mind is susceptible to every impression, whether good or evil, exhibited to its view. The care of education is a work of the highest moment as all the advantages or miscarriages of a man's life are in a great measure dependent on it. It is the duty of parents in particular and friends in general to infuse into the untainted youth early notions of justice and honor so that all possible advantages of good parts may not take an evil turn nor be perverted to base and unworthy purposes.

The mind is to be made obedient to discipline and pliant to reason while it is yet tender and easy to be bowed, but if we suffer ill principles to get ground on infancy, vice to debauch or passion to pervert reason in that unguarded age, when we have once made an ill child, it is a foolish expectation to promise ourselves he will prove a good man. Shall we wonder afterwards to taste the waters bitter when we ourselves have first poisoned the fountain?

Study to be wise and learn to be prudent. Learning is not virtue, but the means to bring us an acquaintance with it. Integrity without knowledge is weak and useless, and knowledge without integrity is dangerous and dreadful. Let these be your motives to action through life: the relief of the distressed, the detections of frauds, the defeat of oppression, and diffusion of happiness. Then shall you appear before God and men like apples of gold in pictures of silver.

Men of great talents by nature and polished by art, if to these accomplishments be added that of a general acquaintance with mankind, are the most dangerous persons to be connected with unless they steadily persevere in the practice of virtue. For they know the secret avenues to the human heart and, having the power to make the worse appear the better reason, we are often betrayed before we conceive ourselves in any danger.

I love you with brotherly love and wish your welfare. My best respects to your whole family.

Nathaniel Greene to Samuel Ward, Jr.
1772

Let your child's first lesson be obedience, and the second may be what you want.

Benjamin Franklin
Poor Richard's Almanac 1739

A great obstacle to good education is the inordinate passion prevalent for novels, and the time lost in that reading which should be instructively employed. When this poison infects the mind, it destroys its time and revolts it against wholesome reading. Reason and fact, plain and unadorned, are rejected. Nothing can engage attention unless dressed in all the figments of fancy, and nothing so bedecked comes amiss. The result is a bloated imagination, sickly judgment, and disgust towards all the real businesses of life. This mass of trash, however, is not without some distinction; some few modelling their narratives, although fictitious, on the incidents of real life, have been able to make them interesting and useful vehicles of sound morality.

Thomas Jefferson to Nathaniel Burwell
1818

Cultivate your mind by the perusal of those books which instruct while they amuse. Do not devote much of your time to novels . . . History, geography, poetry, moral essays, biography, travels, sermons, and other well-written religious productions will not fail to enlarge your understanding, to render you a more agreeable companion, and to exalt your virtue.

Patrick Henry to his daughter Anne

In the Constitution of Spain, as proposed by the late Cortes, there was a principle entirely new to me . . . that no person born after that day should ever acquire the rights of citizenship until he could read and write. It is impossible sufficiently to estimate the wisdom of this provision. Of all those which have been thought of for securing fidelity in the administration of the government, constant reliance to the principles of the constitution, and progressive amendments with the progressive advances of the human mind, or changes in human affairs, it is the most effectual. Enlighten the people generally, and tyranny and oppression of body and mind will vanish . . . although I do not, with some enthusiasts, believe the human condition will ever advance to such a state of perfection as that there shall no longer be pain or vice in the world, yet I believe it susceptible of much improvement . . . and that the diffusion of knowledge among the people is to be the instrument by which it is to be effected. The Constitution of the Cortes had defects enough, but when I saw in it this amendatory provision, I was satisfied all would come right in time under its salutary operation.

Thomas Jefferson to P.S. DuPont de Nemours
1816

While it is universally admitted that a well-instructed people alone can be permanently a free people, and while it is evident that the means of diffusing and improving useful knowledge form so small a proportion of the expenditures for national purposes, I cannot presume it to be unseasonable to invite your attention to the advantages of superadding to the means of education provided by the several States a seminary of learning instituted by the National Legislature within the limits of their exclusive jurisdiction . . .

Such an institution, though local in its legal character, would be universal in its beneficial effects. By enlightening the opinions, by expanding the patriotism, and by assimilating the principles, the sentiments, and the manners of those who might resort to this temple of science, to be redistributed in due time through every part of the community, sources of jealousy and preju-

dice would be diminished, the features of national character would be multiplied, and greater extent given to
social harmony.

James Madison
1810

Knowledge is in every country the surest basis of
public happiness. In one in which the measures of government receive their impressions so immediately from
the sense of the community as in ours it is proportion-
ably essential. To the security of a free constitution it
contributes in various ways—by convincing those who
are entrusted with the public administration that every
valuable end of government is best answered by the
enlightened confidence of the people, and by teaching
the people themselves to know and to value their own
rights; to discern and provide against invasions of them;
to distinguish between oppression and the necessary exercise of lawful authority; between burdens proceeding
from a disregard to their convenience and those resulting from the inevitable exigencies of society; to discrimi-
nate the spirit of liberty from that of licentiousness—
cherishing the first, avoiding the last—and uniting a
speedy but temperate vigilance against encroachments,
with an inviolable respect to the laws.

George Washington
First Annual Address to Congress 1790

The infant mind is pregnant with a variety of passions; But I apprehend it is in the power of those who
are entrusted with the education of youth in a considerable degree to determine the bent of the noble passions
and to fix them on salutary objects, or let them loose to
such as are pernicious or destructive. Here then lies the
foundation of civil liberty; in forming the habits of the
youthful mind, in forwarding every passion that may

tend to the promotion of the happiness of the community, in fixing in ourselves right ideas of benevolence, humanity, integrity and truth. For what purpose to study and letters if they do not render us beneficent and humane?

Nathaniel Greene to Samuel Ward Jr.
1771

Every member of the state, ought diligently to read and study the constitution of his country, and teach the rising generation to be free. By knowing their rights, they will sooner perceive when they are violated, and be the better prepared to defend and assert them.

John Jay
1777

PROPOSALS RELATING
TO THE EDUCATION
OF YOUTH IN PENNSYLVANIA

The good education of youth has been esteemed by wise men in all ages, as the surest foundation of the happiness both of private families and of Commonwealths. Almost all governments have therefore made it a principal object of their attention to establish and endow with proper revenues such seminaries of learning as might supply the succeeding age with men qualified to serve the public with honour to themselves and to their country.

Many of the first settlers of these provinces were men who had received a good education in Europe, and to their wisdom and good management we owe much of our present prosperity. But their hands were full, and they could not do all things. The present race are not thought to be generally of equal ability: For though the American youth are allowed not to want capacity; yet the best capacities require cultivation, it being truly with them, as with the best ground, which unless well tilled and sowed with profitable seed, produces only ranker weeds.

That we may obtain the advantages arising from an increase of knowledge, and prevent as much as may be the mischievous consequences that would attend a general ignorance among us, the following hints are offered towards forming a plan for the education of the youth of Pennsylvania . . .

. . . As to their STUDIES, it would be well if they could be taught everything that is useful, and everything that is ornamental: But art is long, and their time is short. It is therefore proposed that they learn those things that are likely to be most useful and most ornamental. Regard being had to the several professions for which they are intended.

All should be taught to write a fair hand, and swift, as that is useful to all. And with it may be learned something of drawing, by imitation of prints, and some of the first principles of perspective. (Drawing is a kind of universal language, understood by all nations. A man may often express his ideas, even to his own countrymen, more clearly with a lead pencil, or a bit of chalk, than with his tongue. And many can understand a figure, that do not comprehend a description in words, though ever so properly chosen.)

. . . The English language might be taught by grammar; in which some of our best writers, as Tillotson, Addison, Pope, Algernoon Sidney, Cato's Letters, &c. should be classics. (Mr. Locke, speaking of grammar, says, "That to those the greatest part of whose business in this world is to be done with their tongues, and with their pens, it is convenient, if not necessary, that they should speak properly and correctly, whereby they may let their thoughts into other men's minds the more easily, and with the greater impression.")

. . . To form their styles, they should be put on writing letters to each other, making abstracts of what they read; or writing the same things in their own words;

telling or writing stories lately read, in their own ex-
pressions, all to be revised and corrected by the tutor,
who should give his reasons, explain the force and import
of words, &c. (This Mr. Locke recommends, and says,
"The writing of letters has so much to do in all the
occurrences of human life, that no gentleman can avoid
showing himself in this kind of writing. Occasions will
daily force him to make this use of his pen,
which . . . always lays him open to a severer examination
of his breeding, sense and abilities, than oral discourses,
whose transient faults dying for the most part with the
sound that gives them life, and so not subject to a strict
review, more easily escape observation and censure.")

. . . But if HISTORY be made a constant part of
their reading, such as the translations of the Greek and
Roman historians, and the modern histories of ancient
Greece and Rome, &c. may not almost all kinds of useful knowledge be that way introduced to advantage, and
with pleasure to the student? As

GEOGRAPHY, by reading with maps, and being required to point out the places where the greatest actions
were done, to give their old and new names, with the
boundaries, situation, extent of the countries concerned,
&c.

CHRONOLOGY, by the help of Helvicus or some
other writer of the kind, who will enable them to tell
when those events happened; what princes were contemporaries, what states or famous men flourished about
that time, &c. The several principal epochs to be first
well fixed in their memories.

ANCIENT CUSTOMS, religious and civil, being frequently mentioned in history, will give occasion for ex-
plaining them . . .

MORALITY, by discounting and making continual
observations on the causes of the rise or fall of any
man's character, fortune, power, &c. mentioned in history; the advantages of temperance, order, frugality,
industry, perseverance, &c. &c. Indeed the general natural tendency of reading good history, must be, to fix in
the minds of youth deep impressions of the beauty and

usefulness of virtue of all kinds, public spirit, fortitude, &c. (Dr. Turnbull says, "That the useful lessons which ought to be inculcated upon youth, are much better taught and enforced from characters, actions, and events, developing the inward springs of human conduct, and the different consequences of actions, whether with respect to private or public good, than by abstract philosophical lectures.")

. . . History will also afford frequent opportunities of showing the necessity of a public religion, from its usefulness to the public; the advantage of a religious character among private persons; the mischiefs of superstition, &c. and the excellency of the CHRISTIAN RELIGION above all others ancient or modern.

History will also give occasion to expatiate on the advantage of civil orders and Constitutions, how men and their properties are protected by joining in societies and establishing government; their industry encouraged and rewarded, arts invented, and life made more comfortable: The advantages of liberty, mischiefs of licentiousness, benefits arising from good laws and a due execution of justice, &c. Thus may the first principles of sound politics be fixed in the minds of youth. (Thus, as Milton says, should they be instructed in the beginning, end and reasons of political societies; that they may not, in a dangerous fit of the Commonwealth, be such poor, shaken, uncertain reeds, of such a tottering conscience, as many of our great counsellors have lately shown themselves, but steadfast pillars of the state.)

On historical occasions, questions of Right and Wrong, Justice and Injustice, will naturally arise, and may be put to youth, which they may debate in conversation and in writing. (After this, they are to dive into the grounds of law and legal justice; delivered first and with best warrant by Moses; and as far as human prudence can be trusted, in those celebrated remains of the ancient Grecian and Roman lawgivers, &c.) When they ardently desire victory for the sake of the praise attending it, they will begin to feel the want, and be sensible of the use of logic, or the art of reasoning to discover truth, and of arguing to defend it, and convince adversaries . . . Public disputes warm the imagination, whet the industry, and strengthen the natural abilities.

. . . With the whole should be constantly inculcated and cultivated, that Benignity of Mind, which shows itself in searching for and seizing every opportunity to serve and to oblige; and is the foundation of what is called GOOD BREEDING; highly useful to the possessor, and most agreeable to all.

The idea of what is true merit, should also be often presented to youth, explained and impressed on their minds, as consisting in an inclination joined with an ability to serve mankind, one's country, friends and family; which ability is (with the blessing of God) to be acquired or greatly increased by true learning; and should indeed be the great aim and end of all learning. (Mr. Locke says, " 'Tis VIRTUE, then, direct VIRTUE which is to be aimed at in education. All other considerations and accomplishments are nothing in comparison to this. This is the solid and substantial good, which tutors should not only read lectures and talk of, but the labour and art of education should furnish the mind with, and fasten there, and never cease till the young man has a true relish of it, and placed his strength, his glory, and his pleasure in it.")

Benjamin Franklin
1749

7

Gun Control

" . . . the right of the people to keep and bear arms shall not be infringed."

—The Bill of Rights, Article 2

infringe: To break or BREAK DOWN; specif.: a. To destroy. b. TO FRUSTRATE. c. TO IMPAIR.

Over two hundred years ago, in "The Federalist Papers," James Madison unwittingly prophesied the absurd principle behind the push for government control of firearms. "Liberty is to faction, what air is to fire," he stated, " a nutrient without which it instantly expires. But it could not be a less folly to abolish liberty, which is essential to political life, because it nourishes faction, than it would be to wish the annihilation of air, which is essential to life, because it imparts to fire its destructive agency."

What Madison could not foresee, however, was the astounding moral decline that would virtually guarantee such an attempt to abolish our liberties (one of which is found in the second amendment to the Bill of Rights). Concerning this, Edmund Burke warned, "Society cannot exist unless a controlling power upon will and appetite be placed somewhere, and the less of it there is within, the more there must be without." The banning of guns is no answer; it is only proof that there is a problem. The outward is replacing the inward. The abolition of man's God-given liberty is inevitable wherever man's God-given inward restraints are cast off. If the moral vacuum of this present era continues, we must expect, as a matter of course, to see our constitutional birthright being stripped from us. It cannot be otherwise. The preceding chapter, in referring to "direct virtue" in education, has provided us with something gun control never can; an answer to a very serious problem.

Forty years ago, when the resolution of enslaving America was formed in Great Britain, the British parliament was advised by an artful man, (Sir William Keith) who was governor of Pennsylvania, to disarm the people; that it was the best and most effectual way to enslave them; but that they should not do it openly.

George Mason
1788

No free man shall be debarred the use of arms within his own land.

Thomas Jefferson
Virginia Constitution 1776

A free people ought not only to be armed, but disciplined.

George Washington
First Annual Address to Congress 1790

They that can give up essential liberty to purchase a little temporary safety deserve neither liberty nor safety.

Benjamin Franklin
1759

None but an armed nation can dispense with a standing army.

Thomas Jefferson
1803

Guard with jealous attention the public liberty. Suspect everyone who approaches that jewel. Unfortunately, nothing will preserve it but downright force. Whenever you give up that force you are ruined.

Patrick Henry
Virginia Ratifying Convention 1787-1788

Americans (have) the right and advantage of being armed—Unlike citizens of other countries whose governments are afraid to trust the people with arms.

James Madison
The Federalist #46

The peaceable part of mankind will be continually overrun by the vile and abandoned while they neglect the means of self defense . . . Weakness allures the ruffian (but) arms, like laws, discourage and keep the invader and plunderer in awe, and preserve order in the world . . . horrid mischief would ensue were (the good) deprived of the use of them.

Thomas Paine

Those who recollect the distress and danger to this country in former periods from the lack of arms, must exult in the assurance from their representatives, that we shall soon rival foreign countries, not only in the number, but in the quality of arms, completed from our own manufacturers.

John Adams
Address to House of Representatives

The constitutions of most of our states assert, that all power is inherent in the people; that they may exercise it by themselves, in all cases to which they think themselves competent, or they may act by representatives, freely and equally chosen; that it is their right and duty to be at all times armed.

Thomas Jefferson to Major John Cartwright
1824

To be prepared for war is one of the most effectual
means of preserving peace.

George Washington
First Annual Address to Congress 1790

8

Welfare

" . . . you offered a premium for the encouragement of idleness, and you should not now wonder that it has had its effect in the increase of poverty . . ."

—Benjamin Franklin

"We have the right, as individuals, to give away as much of our own money as we please in charity; but as members of Congress we have no right to appropriate a dollar of the public money." Thus spoke legendary U.S. congressman, Davy Crockett. He understood the ethical contradiction we face today. Justification for the welfare state rests on this flawed premise: Good feelings are morally superior to good deeds. For some, the former (compassion) may underlie welfare, but the latter (benevolence)? Never. Welfare is just not a good deed. It is actually sinister in a number of ways:

1. It rewards and encourages idleness, *thus undermining our national prosperity.*

2. Its continued existence depends upon lies, *sidestepping our good sense while exploiting our good feelings.*

3. It is theft. *Soviet dictator, Joseph Stalin, described his socialistic ideology in these terms: "From each according to his ability; to each according to his need." The welfare system is just such an arrangement. Person A (the socialist authority) takes from B and gives to C. This obtains for A the moral high ground AND a position of perpetuated power. In truth, government welfare is an unconstitutional, yet legal, system of confiscating legitimately acquired wealth under the guise of helping the needy. No wonder the federal government insists on such compassion. As dependence is increased by this means, federal power is expanded.*

If the "compassionate" could acquire a disposition to do good with their OWN resources rather than those of OTHERS, they would enter the ranks of the truly benevolent who do not talk much of doing good as they are too busy in the practice of it. Perhaps, after all, this is what Congressman Crockett meant.

As long as the products of our labor, and the rewards of our care, can properly be called our own, so
long it will be worth our while to be industrious and
frugal. But if when we plow—sow—reap—gather—and
thresh—we find that we plow—sow—reap—gather—and
thresh for others, whose PLEASURE is to be the SOLE
LIMITATION how much they shall take, and how much
they shall leave, WHY should we repeat the unprofitable
toil?

John Dickinson
Letters from a Pennsylvania Farmer

The poor, unable to support themselves, are maintained by an assessment on the titheable persons in their
parish. This assessment is levied and administered by
twelve persons in each parish, called vestrymen, origi-
nally chosen by the housekeepers of the parish, but afterwards filling vacancies in their own body by their own
choice. These are usually the most discreet farmers, so
distributed through their parish, that every part of it
may be under the immediate eye of some one of them.
They are well acquainted with the details and economy
of private life, and they find sufficient inducements to
execute their charge well, in their philanthropy, in the
approbation of their neighbors, and the distinction which
that gives them. The poor who have neither property,
friends, nor strength to labor, are boarded in the houses
of good farmers, to whom a stipulated sum is annually
paid. To those who are able to help themselves a little,
or have friends from whom they derive some succours,
inadequate however to their full maintenance, supple-
mentary aids are given, which enable them to live com-
fortably in their own houses, or in the houses of their
friends. Vagabonds, without visible property or voca-
tion, are placed in workhouses, where they are well
clothed, fed, lodged, and made to labor. Nearly the
same method for providing for the poor prevails through
all our states; and from Savannah to Portsmouth you

will seldom meet a beggar. In the larger towns, indeed, they sometimes present themselves. These are usually foreigners, who have never obtained a settlement in any parish. I never yet saw a native American begging in the streets or highways. A subsistence is easily gained here: and if, by misfortunes, they are thrown on the charities of the world, those provided by their own country are so comfortable and so certain, that they never think of relinquishing them to become strolling beggars.

Thomas Jefferson
Notes on Virginia 1782

Here everyone may have land to labor for himself if he chooses; or, preferring the exercise of any other industry, may exact for it such compensation as not only to afford a comfortable subsistence, but wherewith to provide for a cessation from labor in old age.

Thomas Jefferson to John Adams
1813

Let your promotion result from your own application and from intrinsic merit, not from the labors of others. The last would prove fallacious, and expose you to reproach of the daw in borrowed feathers.

George Washington to George Washington Parke Custis
1796

I think the best way of doing good to the poor, is not making them easy in poverty, but leading or driving them out of it. In my youth I travelled much, and I observed in different countries, that the more public provisions were made for the poor, the less they provided for themselves, and of course became poorer. And, on the contrary, the less was done for them, the more they did for themselves, and became richer. There is no country in the world where so many provisions are established for them (as in Great Britain) ... Under all these obligations, are our poor modest, humble, and thankful; and do they use their best endeavours to maintain themselves, and lighten our shoulders of this burden?—On the contrary, I affirm that there is no country in the world in which the poor are more idle, dissolute, drunken, and insolent. The day you passed that act, you took away from before their eyes the greatest of all inducements to industry, frugality, and sobriety, by giving them a dependence on somewhat else than a careful accumulation during youth and health, for support in age or sickness. In short, you offered a premium for the encouragement of idleness, and you should not now wonder that it has had its effect in the increase of poverty. Repeal that law, and you will soon see a change in their manners. St. Monday, and St. Tuesday, will cease to be holidays. SIX days shalt thou labour, though one of the old commandments long treated as out of date, will again be looked upon as a respectable precept; industry will increase, and with it plenty among the lower people; their circumstances will mend, and more will be done for their happiness by inuring them to provide for themselves, than could be done by dividing all your estates among them.

Benjamin Franklin
The London Chronicle 1766

I fear the giving mankind a dependence on anything for support in age or sickness, besides industry and frugality during youth and health, tends to flatter our natural indolence, to encourage idleness and prodigality, and thereby to promote and increase poverty, the very evil it was intended to cure; thus multiplying beggars, instead of diminishing them.

Benjamin Franklin
Gentleman's Magazine 1768

9

Term Limits

". . . they were at a certain period to . . . become the governed instead of the governor, which might still keep alive that regard to the public good . . ."

—*Thomas Jefferson*

Prepare for another spirited debate! Following in the style of chapter 3 (and 5 to a lesser degree), the following dialogue contains potent artillery—a scintillating array of well-reasoned opinions, fired out upon the ageless philosophical battlefield. The principal warriors once again fall in line under two opposing banners: ENERGETIC versus LIMITED government.

James Madison, who "fathered" the Constitution, fought strenuously against term limits in the Senate, citing the need for firmness, consistency, and experience in defense of his argument. In approaching the House of Representatives, however, he launches a brilliant offensive that strikes at the common sense of us all.

". . . the members of the Federal legislature will be likely to attach themselves too much to local objects . . . Measures will too often be decided according to their probable effect, not on the national prosperity and happiness, but on the prejudices, interests and pursuits of the governments and people of the individual states." (The Federalist no.46)

200 years later, the crusaders have changed, but the arguments remain much the same, suggesting the controversy may perhaps never be reconciled. Nevertheless it continues inexorably, for we cannot resist the free expression of thought.

Nothing is so essential to the preservation of a republican government as a periodical rotation. Nothing so strongly impels a man to regard the interest of his constituents, as the certainty of returning to the general mass of the people, from whence he was taken, where he must participate in their burdens. It is a great defect in the Senate that they are not ineligible at the end of six years . . . At the end of that long term (they) may again be elected. What will be the operation of this? Is it not probable, that those gentlemen who will be elected senators will fix themselves in the federal town, and become citizens of that town more than of (their) state? They will purchase a good seat in or near the town, and become inhabitants of that place . . . They will be a continually existing body. They will exercise those machinations and contrivances, which the many have always to fear from the few . . . The senators living at the spot will feel no inconvenience from long sessions, as they will vote themselves handsome pay, without incurring any additional expenses.

George Mason
Virginia Ratifying Convention 1788

There is no provision (in the Constitution) for a rotation, nor anything to prevent the perpetuity of office in the same hands for life; which by a little well timed bribery, will probably be done, to the exclusion of men of the best abilities from their share in the offices of government.—By this neglect we lose the advantages of that check to the overbearing insolence of office, which by rendering him ineligible at certain periods, keeps the mind of man in equilibria, and teaches him the feelings of the governed, and better qualifies him to govern in his turn.

Elbridge Gerry
1788

Sir, in contending for a rotation, the gentlemen carry their zeal beyond all reasonable bounds. I am convinced that no government, founded on this feeble principle, can operate well . . . The gentlemen deceive themselves— The amendment would defeat their own design. When a man knows he must quit his station, let his merit be what it may; he will turn his attention chiefly to his own emolument: Nay, he will feel temptations, which few other situations furnish; to perpetuate his power by unconstitutional usurpations.

Alexander Hamilton
New York Ratifying Convention 1788

The mutability in the public councils, arising from a rapid succession of new members, however qualified they may be, points out in the strongest manner, the necessity of some stable institution in the government. Every new election in the states is found to change one half of the representatives. From this change of men must proceed a change of opinions; and from a change of opinions, a change of measures. But a continual change even of good measures is inconsistent with every rule of prudence, and every prospect of success . . . (The Senate ought, therefore) to possess great firmness, and consequently ought to hold its authority by a tenure of considerable duration.

James Madison
The Federalist #62 1788

Government will always take its complexion from the habits of the people—habits are continually changing from age to age—a body of legislators taken from the people, will generally represent these habits at the time when they are chosen—hence these two important conclusions, 1st: That a legislative body should be frequently renewed and always taken from the people— 2nd: That a government which is perpetual, or incapable of being accommodated to every change of national habits, must in time become a bad government.

Noah Webster
American Magazine 1788

In the commencement of a revolution, which received its birth from the usurpations of tyranny, nothing was more natural, than that the public mind should be influenced by an extreme spirit of jealousy. To resist these encroachments, and to nourish this spirit, was the great object of all our public and private institutions. The zeal for liberty became predominant and excessive. In forming our confederation, this passion alone seemed to actuate us, and we appear to have had no other view than to secure ourselves from despotism. The object certainly was a valuable one, and deserved our utmost attention; But, Sir, there is another object, equally important, and which our enthusiasm rendered us little capable of regarding—I mean a principle of strength and stability in the organization of our government, and vigor in its operations. This purpose could never be accomplished but by the establishment of some select body, formed peculiarly upon this principle. There are few positions more demonstrable than that there should be in every republic, some permanent body to correct the prejudices, check the intemperate passions, and regulate the fluctuations of a popular assembly . . .

Alexander Hamilton
New York Ratifying Convention 1788

It is certainly inconsistent with the established principles of republicanism, that the senate should be a fixed and unchangeable body of men. There should be then some constitutional provision against this evil. A rotation I consider as the best possible mode of affecting a remedy. The amendment will not only have a tendency to defeat any plots, which may be formed against the liberty and authority of the state governments, but will be the best means to extinguish the factions which often prevail, and which are sometimes so fatal to legislative bodies. This appears to me an important consideration. We have generally found, that perpetual bodies have either combined in some scheme of usurpation, or have been torn and distracted with cabals—Both have been the source of misfortunes to the state. Most people acquainted with history will acknowledge these facts . . . I think a rotation in the government is a very important and truly republican institution . . .

Melancton Smith
New York Ratifying Convention 1788

It is an unquestionable truth, that the body of the people in every country desire sincerely its prosperity: But it is equally unquestionable, that they do not possess the discernment and stability necessary for systematic government. To deny that they are frequently led into the grossest errors by misinformation and passion, would be a flattery which their own good sense must despise . . .

Sir, if you consider but a moment the purposes, for which the senate was instituted, and the nature of the business which they are to transact, you will see the necessity of giving them duration. They, together with the President, are to manage all our concerns with foreign nations: They must understand all their interests, and their political systems. This knowledge is not soon acquired—But a very small part is gained in the closet. Is it desirable then that new and unqualified members should be continually thrown into that body? When public bodies are engaged in the exercise of general powers, you cannot judge of the propriety of their conduct, but from the result of their systems. They may be forming plans, which require time and diligence to bring to maturity. It is necessary, therefore, that they should have a considerable and fixed duration, that they may make their calculations accordingly. If they are to be perpetu-ally fluctuating, they can never have that responsibility which is so important in republican governments.

Alexander Hamilton
New York Ratifying Convention 1788

. . . If I recollect right, it was observed by an honor-able member from New York, that this amendment would be an infringement of the natural rights of the people. I humbly conceive, if the gentleman reflects maturely on the nature of his argument, he will acknowledge its weakness. What is government itself, but a restraint upon the natural rights of the people? What constitution was ever devised, that did not operate as a restraint on their original liberties? What is the whole system of qualifica-tions, which take place in all free governments, but a restraint? Why is a certain age made necessary? Why a certain term of citizenship? This constitution itself, Sir, has restraints innumerable.—The amendment, it is true, may exclude two of the best men: but it can rarely hap-pen, that the state will sustain any material loss by this. I hope and believe that we shall always have more than two men, who are capable of discharging the duty of a senator.

Melancton Smith
New York Ratifying Convention 1788

It has been observed, that it is not possible there should be in a state only two men qualified for senators. But, sir, the question is not, whether there may be no more than two men; but whether, in certain emergen-cies, you could find two equal to those whom the amend-ment would discard. Important negotiations, or other business to which they shall be most competent, may employ them, at the moment of their removal. These things often happen. The difficulty of obtaining men,

capable of conducting the affairs of a nation in dangerous times, is much more serious than the gentlemen
imagine.

Alexander Hamilton
New York Ratifying Convention 1788

To make (the Senate of Virginia) independent, I
had proposed that they should hold their places for
nine years, and then go out (one third every three years)
and be incapable forever of being re-elected to that
house. My idea was that if they might be re-elected, they
would be casting their eye forward to the period of election (however distant) and be currying favor with the
electors, and consequently dependent on them. My reason for fixing them in office for a term of years rather
than for life, was that they might have in idea that they
were at a certain period to return into the mass of the
people and become the governed instead of the governor, which might still keep alive that regard to the public
good that otherwise they might perhaps be induced by
their independence to forget.

Thomas Jefferson to Edmund Pendleton
1776

10

Religion

*" . . . with a firm reliance on the
protection of Divine Providence . . ."*

—The Declaration of Independence

Decades ago, General Douglas MacArthur warned, "History fails to record a single precedent in which nations subject to moral decay have not passed into political and economic decline. There has been either a spiritual awakening to overcome the moral lapse, or a progressive deterioration leading to ultimate national disaster."

Centuries ago, President George Washington said, "Of all the dispositions and habits which lead to political prosperity, religion and morality are indespensable supports."

Millenniums ago, King Solomon wrote, "Righteousness exalts a nation, but sin is a reproach to any people."

There have, of course, been sentiments to the contrary: "The first requisite for the people's happiness is the abolition of religion." This is from the pen of Karl Marx.

Of all the dispositions and habits which lead to political prosperity, religion and morality are indespensable supports. In vain would that man claim the tribute of patriotism who should labor to subvert these great pillars of human happiness—these firmest props of the duties of men and citizens. The mere politician, equally with the pious man, ought to respect and to cherish them. A volume could not trace all their connections with private and public felicity. Whatever may be conceded to the influence of refined education on minds of peculiar structure, reason and experience both forbid us to expect that national morality can prevail in exclusion of religious principle. It is substantially true that virtue or morality is a necessary spring of popular government.

George Washington
Farewell Address 1796

As medicines sometimes lie many days or weeks in the body without being felt, and before they take effect, so does moral and religious instruction. Years after being administered it produces good effects.

Benjamin Rush
1798

After all, my dear friend, do not imagine that I am vain enough to ascribe our success (in the Revolutionary War) to any superiority . . . I am too well acquainted with all the springs and levers of our machine, not to see, that our human means were unequal to our undertaking, and that, if it had not been for the justice of our cause, and the consequent interposition of providence, in which we had faith, we must have been ruined. If I had ever before been an atheist, I should now have been convinced of the being and government of a Deity! It is he who abases the proud and favours the humble. May we never forget his goodness to us, and may our future conduct manifest our gratitude.

Benjamin Franklin to William Strahan
1784

Statesmen, my dear Sir, may plan and speculate for liberty, but it is religion and morality alone, which can establish the principles upon which freedom can securely stand. The only foundation of a free constitution is pure virtue; and if this cannot be inspired into our people in a greater measure than they have it now, they may change their rulers and the forms of government, but they will not obtain a lasting liberty. They will only exchange tyrants and tyrannies.

John Adams to Zabdiel Adams
1776

Adequate security (in the Constitution) is also given to the rights of conscience and private judgment. They are, by nature, subject to no control but that of the Deity, and in that free situation they are now left. Every man is permitted to consider, to adore and to worship his Creator in the manner most agreeable to his conscience. No opinions are dictated; no rules of faith prescribed; no preference given to one sect to the prejudice of others.—The constitution, however, has wisely declared, that the "liberty of Conscience, thereby granted, shall not be so construed as to excuse acts of licentiousness, or justify practices inconsistent with the peace or safety of this state." In a word, the convention, by whom that constitution was formed, were of opinion, that the gospel of Christ, like the ark of God, would not fall, though unsupported by the arm of flesh; and happy would it be for mankind, if that opinion prevailed more generally.

John Jay
1777

There seems to be a disposition in men to find fault, rather than to act as they ought. The works of creation itself have been objected to: and one learned prince declared, that if he had been consulted, they would have been improved. With what book has so much fault been found, as with the Bible? Perhaps, principally, because it so clearly and strongly enjoins men to do right. How many, how plausible objections have been made against it, with how much ardor, with how much pains? Yet, the book has done more good than all the books in the world; would do much more, if duly regarded; and might lead the objectors against it to happiness, if they would value it as they should.

John Dickinson
Letters of Fabius #4 1788

Direct my thoughts, words and work, wash away my sins in the immaculate Blood of the Lamb, and purge my heart by Thy Holy Spirit . . . daily frame me more and more into the likeness of Thy Son Jesus Christ.

George Washington
1752

The early part of my life was spent in dissipation, folly, and in the practice of some of the vices to which young men are prone. The weight of that folly and those vices has been felt in my mind ever since. They have often been deplored in tears and sighs before God. It was from deep and affecting sense of one of them that I was first led to seek the favor of God in his Son in the 21st year of my age. . . .

The religious impressions that were made upon my mind at this time were far from issuing in a complete union to God by his Son Jesus Christ, but they left my mind more tender to sin of every kind, and begat in me

constant desires for a new heart, and a sense of God's
mercy in the way of his Gospel.

Benjamin Rush
from Autobiography

Amongst other strange things said of me, I hear it
is said by the deists that I am one of the number; and,
indeed, that some good people think I am no Christian.
This thought gives me much more pain than the appel-
lation of Tory; because I think religion of infinitely higher
importance than politics; and I find much cause to reproach myself that I have lived so long, and have given
no decided and public proofs of my being a Christian.
But, indeed, My dear child, this is a character which I
prize far above all this world has, or can boast.

Patrick Henry to daughter
1796

The safety and prosperity of nations ultimately and
essentially depend on the protection and blessing of
Almighty God; and the national acknowledgment of this
truth is not only an indispensable duty, which the people
owe to him, but a duty whose natural influence is favorable to the promotion of that morality and piety, without which social happiness cannot exist, nor the blessings of a free government be enjoyed.

John Adams
Proclamation for a National Fast 1798

I now make it my earnest prayer that God . . . would
graciously be pleased to dispose us all to do justice, to
love mercy, and to conduct ourselves with charity and
humility, and a pacific temper of mind, which were char-
acteristics of the Divine Author of our blessed religion,

and without a humble imitation of whose example in these things, we can never hope to be a happy nation.

George Washington
Letter to Governors 1783

He is the best friend to American liberty, who is most sincere and active in promoting true and undefiled religion, and who sets himself with the greatest firmness to bear down on profanity and immorality of every kind. Whoever is an avowed enemy of God, I scruple not to call him an enemy to his country.

John Witherspoon
1776

Truth, honor, and religion are the only foundation to build human happiness upon. They never fail to yield a mind solid satisfaction; For conscious virtue gives pleasure to the soul.

Nathaniel Greene to Catharine Ward Greene
1776

Whereas it is the duty of all nations to acknowledge the providence of Almighty God, to obey His will, to be grateful for His benefits, and humbly to implore His protection and favor; and

Whereas both Houses of Congress have, by their joint committee requested me "to recommend to the people of the United States a day of public thanksgiving and prayer, to be observed by acknowledging with grateful hearts the many and signal favors of Almighty God, especially by affording them an opportunity peaceably to establish a form of government for their safety and happiness:"

Now, therefore, I do recommend and assign Thursday, the 26th day of November next, to be devoted by the people of these States to the service of that great and glorious Being who is the beneficent author of all the good that was, that is, or that will be; that we may then all unite in rendering unto Him our sincere and humble thanks for His kind care and protection of the people of this country previous to their becoming a nation; for the signal and manifold mercies and the favorable interpositions of His providence in the course and conclusion of the late war; for the great degree of tranquillity, union, and plenty which we have since enjoyed; for the peaceable and rational manner in which we have been enabled to establish constitutions of government for our safety and happiness, and particularly the national one now lately instituted; for the civil and religious liberty with which we are blessed, and the means we have of acquiring and diffusing useful knowledge; and, in general, for all the great and various favors which He has been pleased to confer upon us.

And also that we may then unite in most humbly offering our prayers and supplications to the great Lord and Ruler of Nations, and beseech Him to pardon our national and other transgressions; to enable us all, whether in public or private stations, to perform our several and relative duties properly and punctually; to render our national government a blessing to all the people by constantly being a government of wise, just, and constitutional laws, discreetly and faithfully executed and obeyed; to protect and guide all sovereigns and nations (especially such as have shown kindness to us), and to bless them with good governments, peace, and concord; to promote the knowledge and practice of true religion and virtue, and the increase of science among them and us; and, generally, to grant unto all mankind such a degree of temporal prosperity as He alone knows to be best. Given under my hand, at the city of New York, the 3rd day of October, A.D. 1789.

George Washington
Thanksgiving Day Proclamation 1789

Opinions, for a long time, have been gradually gaining ground, which threaten the foundations of religion,
morality and society. An attack was first made upon the
Christian revelation; for which natural religion was offered as the substitute. The Gospel was to be discarded
as a gross imposture; but the being and attributes of a
GOD, the obligations of piety, even the doctrine of a
future state of rewards and punishments were to be retained and cherished.

In proportion as success has appeared to attend the
plan, a bolder project has been unfolded. The very existence of a Deity has been questioned, and in some
instances denied. The duty of piety has been ridiculed,
the perishable nature of man asserted and his hopes
bounded to the short span of his earthly state. DEATH
has been proclaimed an ETERNAL SLEEP—"the dogma
of the immortality of the soul a cheat invented to tor-
ment the living for the benefit of the dead." Irreligion,
no longer confined to the closets of conceiled sophists,
nor to the haunts of wealthy riot, has more or less displayed its hideous front among all classes.

Alexander Hamilton
1794

I tremble for my country when I reflect that God is
just.

Thomas Jefferson
Notes on Virginia 1782

In the course of (a party) one of them asked me if
I believed in Christ? I answered that I did, and that I
thanked God that I did . . . (A physician) during one of
his visits very abruptly remarked that there was no God,
and he hoped the time would come when there would
be no religion in the world. I very concisely remarked
that if there was no God, there could be no moral ob-

ligations, and I did not see how society could exist without them. He did not hesitate to admit that, if there was no God, there could be no moral obligations, but insisted that they were not necessary, for that society would find a substitute for them in enlightened self-interest. I soon turned the conversation to another topic, and he, probably perceiving that his sentiments met with a cold reception, did not afterward resume the subject.

John Jay
1822

We have no government armed with power capable of contending with human passions unbridled by morality and religion. Avarice, ambition, revenge, or gallantry, would break the strongest cords of our Constitution as a whale goes through a net. Our Constitution was made only for a moral and religious people. It is wholly inadequate to the government of any other.

John Adams
1798

No people can be bound to acknowledge and adore the Invisible Hand which conducts the affairs of men more than those of the United States. Every step by which they have advanced to the character of an independent nation seems to have been distinguished by some token of providential agency.

George Washington
First Inaugural Address 1789

In this situation of this Assembly, groping, as it were, in the dark to find political truth, and scarcely able to distinguish it when presented to us, how has it happened, Sir, that we have not hitherto once thought of humbly applying to the Father of Lights to illuminate our understandings: In the beginning of the contest with Britain, when we were sensible of danger, we had daily prayers in this room for the Divine Protection. Our prayers, Sir, were heard;—and they were graciously answered. All of us, who were engaged in the Struggle, must have observed frequent instances of a superintending Providence in our favour. To that kind Providence we owe this happy opportunity of consulting in peace on the means of establishing our future national felicity. And have we now forgotten that powerful Friend? Or do we imagine we no longer need his assistance? I have lived, Sir, a long time; and the longer I live, the more convincing proofs I see of this Truth, that GOD governs in the affairs of men. And if a sparrow cannot fall to the ground without his notice, is it probable that an Empire can rise without his aid? We have been assured, Sir, in the Sacred Writings, that "except the Lord build the house, they labour in vain that build it." I firmly believe this; and I also believe, that without his concurring aid, we shall succeed in this political building no better than the builders of Babel; we shall be divided by our little, partial, local interests, our projects will be confounded, and we ourselves shall become a reproach and a byeword down to future ages. And what is worse, mankind may hereafter, from this unfortunate instance, despair of establishing government by human wisdom, and leave it to chance, war, and conquest. I therefore beg leave to move, that henceforth, prayers imploring the assistance of Heaven and its blessing on our deliberations, be held in this Assembly every morning before we proceed to business.

Benjamin Franklin
from speech in the Constitutional Convention 1787

PART TWO

-Sketches-

CHAPTER TWO

1
John Adams
1735-1826

"The Atlas of American Independence," was one of the most industrious figures throughout the revolutionary struggle and the establishing of the new nation. John Adams was the second president of the United States as well as the first vice-president under George Washington. Regarding the latter position, he once wrote to his wife, "My country has, in its wisdom, contrived for me the most insignificant office that ever the invention of man contrived or his imagination conceived."

Adams was a revolutionary ahead of his time. When reconciliation with Great Britain was still the hope of most colonial leaders, he called for separation as the only means to a national happiness. "He was a most sensible and forcible speaker," wrote Benjamin Rush, "He was equally fearless of men, and of the consequences of a bold assertion of his opinion in all his speeches . . . Every member of Congress in 1776 acknowledged him to be the first man in the House . . . He was a stranger to dissimulation, and appeared to be more jealous of his reputation for integrity than for talents or knowledge. He was strictly moral, and at all times respectful to Religion." He did not, however, possess the warmer human qualities that make a man popular. He was vain and stubborn, only seeing in black and white. And while he was greatly admired for his courageous spirit, he was not greatly loved.

Abigail Adams was of inestimable support to her husband's labors, as well as a patriot of comparable proportions. She once wrote, "Our cause, Sir, I trust, is the cause of truth and justice and will finally prevail, though the combined force of earth and hell should rise against it."

Adams' strict sense of justice led him, in the face of popular opinion, to defend the British soldiers arrested for the murder of five colonists in the Boston Massacre of 1770. He argued that the rioting colonists were a threat to the soldiers' safety and therefore they were justified in defending themselves. Though he kindled the immediate rage of his countrymen, he displayed to future generations that impartial judgement and integrity which fame could not buy.

In 1776, Adams was appointed by Congress to a committee of five men, including Thomas Jefferson, Benjamin Franklin, Roger Sherman, and Robert R. Livingston. Their task was to draw up a declaration of independence. Adams himself gives the following account:

The committee met, discussed the subject, and then appointed Mr. Jefferson and me to make the draught, I suppose because we were the two first on the list.

The sub-committee met. Jefferson proposed to me to make the draught.

> *I said, "I will not."*
> *"You should do it."*
> *"Oh! no."*
> *"Why will you not? You ought to do it."*
> *"I will not."*
> *"Why?"*
> *"Reason enough."*
> *"What can be your reasons?"*

"Reason first—You are a Virginian, and a Virginian ought to appear at the head of this business. Reason second—I am obnoxious, suspected and unpopular. You are very much otherwise. Reason third—You can write ten times better than I can."

"Well," said Jefferson, "if you are decided, I will do as well as I can."

For many years after his presidency ended, Adams was bitter over what he felt was slanderous and malicious treatment by many, including Jefferson, his former vice-president. The warm friendship that had existed between them during their early years was to suffer a prolonged period of silence. After they were both retired from public life, their old friendship was restored and they enjoyed a long season of correspondence. On July 4, 1826, exactly fifty years after the Declaration of Independence was signed, John Adams died. His last words were, "Thomas Jefferson still survives!" He did not know that only hours before, that same morning, Jefferson had died at Monticello.

2
Samuel Adams
1722-1803

Thirteen years the elder of his cousin, the second president, Samuel Adams, was the spark that lit the flame of the American struggle for independence. The historian George Bancroft called him, "the helmsman of the Revolution at its origin." Organizer of the patriotic society, the "Sons of Liberty," with outlaws such as Paul Revere and John Hancock, Adams was considered a traitor against the crown. He instigated the Boston Tea Party and once declared that even if it was revealed to him that 999 out of 1000 men would die in a war for liberty, he would still favor it rather than see the nation enslaved. The few survivors would "propagate a nation of freemen."

Appearing aged before his time, Adams' body shook slightly when he stood to speak. Even so, he possessed a healthy and muscular frame. With eyes of clear gray, his face was capable of great expression. As to his manner of speaking, Thomas Jefferson writes, "Mr. Samuel Adams, although not of fluent elocution, was so rigorously logical, so clear in his views, abundant in good sense, and master always of his subject, that he commanded the most profound attention whenever he rose in an assembly." And again, "I always considered him more than any other member, the fountain of our more important issues." Benjamin Rush painted the firebrand's character thus:

He loved simplicity and economy in the administration of government, and despised the appeals which are made to the eyes and ears of the common people in order to govern them. He considered national happiness and the public patronage of religion as inseparably connected; and so great was his regard for public worship, as the means of promoting religion, that he constantly attended divine service in the German church in

York town while the Congress sat there, when there was no service in their chapel, although he was ignorant of the German language. His morals were irreproachable, and even ambition and avarice, the usual vices of politicians, seemed to have no place in his breast.

Adams as a central figure diminished greatly as the end of the war ushered in the establishment of the new Republic. His vehemently against centralized power severely limited his ability, not to mention his willingness, to contribute to just such a government. Nevertheless he eventually gave his blessing to the new Constitution, and urged its ratification in his home state of Massachusetts, provided a Bill of Rights would be added.

When the Anti-Federalist administration of Jefferson came to the White House at the turn of the century, the third President wrote to his old friend, now 79 years old, "How much I lament that time has deprived me of your aid! It would have been a day of glory which should have called you to the first office of my administration. But give us your counsel, my friend, and give us your blessing, and be assured that there exists not in the heart of man a more faithful esteem than mine to you, and that I shall ever bear you the most affectionate veneration and respect."

Adams' Biographer, James K. Hosmer, reveals in the following story the warmth of devotion with which the aged "Cromwell of New England" was regarded in his closing years:

When, in 1800, Governor Caleb Strong was advancing through Winter Street, in a great procession, probably at the time of his inauguration, Mr. Adams was observed in his house, looking out upon the pageant. The governor called a halt, and ordered the music to cease. Alighting from his carriage, he greeted the old man at the door, grasped the paralytic hands, and expressed, with head bared, his reverence for Samuel Adams. The soldiers presented arms, and the people stood uncovered and silent.

3
Ethan Allen
1737-1789

At dawn on May 10, 1775, less than a month into the Revolutionary War, Ethan Allen, an untamed backwoods patriot from Connecticut, and his Green Mountain Boys prepared for a daring attack on Fort Ticonderoga. "Friends and fellow soldiers," announced Allen, "You have, for a number of years past, been a scourge and a terror to arbitrary power . . . I now propose to advance before you and, in person, conduct you through the wicket-gate; for we must this morning either quit our pretensions to valor or possess ourselves of this fortress in a few minutes; and, inasmuch as it is a desperate attempt, which none but the bravest of men dare undertake, I do not urge it on any contrary to his will. You that will undertake voluntarily, poise your firelocks." And with that, he and his men burst into the fort, catching the commander just out of bed with breeches still in hand. Allen bore down on him with extraordinary severity, demanding the surrender of the fort. When asked by what authority he did so, his immortal reply was, "In the name of the Great Jehovah and the Continental Congress." With a drawn sword over his head, the commander surrendered, thus giving America her first victory of the war. Allen wrote that "the sun seemed to rise that morning with a superior luster, and Ticonderoga . . . smiled on its conquerors."

Ethan Allen was a man of great physical prowess. He was unrefined to be sure, but self-reliant, and confident in his ability to conquer tyranny. A fellow patriot described him thus:

He used to show a fracture in one of his teeth, occasioned by his twisting off with it, in a fit of anger, the nail which fastened the bar of his handcuffs; and which drew from one of the astonished spectators the exclamation of "damn him, can he eat iron?"... I have seldom met with a man possessing, in my opinion, a stronger mind, or whose mode of expression was more vehement and oratorical. His style was a singular compound of local barbarisms, Scriptural phrases, and oriental wildness; and though unclassic and sometimes ungrammatical, it was highly animated and forcible."

The handcuffs mentioned refer to the three-year period which began shortly after the victory at Fort Ticonderoga, when Allen was imprisoned after being captured during a campaign in Montreal. Upon his release in 1778, he immediately reported to George Washington at Valley Forge and was made a Colonel in the Continental Army "in reward of his fortitude, firmness and zeal in the cause of his country, manifested during his long and cruel captivity, as well as on former occasions."

The brief, but dynamic career of Ethan Allen was marred near the end of the war by his attempt to unite his adopted state of Vermont with Canada as a British Province. He was accused of treason, but his guilt was never proved, though it was apparent he was devoted more to his state than to the blossoming Union. Nevertheless, a marble statue of the Captor of Ticonderoga stands today in Statuary Hall in the Capitol of the United States of America.

4
John Dickinson
1732-1808

Called the "Penman of the Revolution," John Dickinson fanned the flames of independence through his stirring essays on the eve of the Revolution. He was author of the original Articles of Confederation, the Olive Branch Petition, and the widely circulated series of articles, "Letters from a Farmer in Pennsylvania," which exposed the despotic nature of the British tax laws in the colonies. He was a signer of the Constitution and effectively utilized his talents in defending it in his "Letters of Fabius." George Washington said he was a "master of his subject, he treats it with dignity, and at the same time expresses himself in such a manner as to render it intelligent to every capacity." And Thomas Jefferson's estimate was that "nobody's judgement is entitled to more respect than Mr. Dickinson's when truly informed of facts, nor does anybody respect it more than Thomas Jefferson."

Tall and slender in build, with clear eyes and a prominent nose, Dickinson was extraordinarily well read in philosophy, law, and classical literature. He was extremely analytical, and rarely emotional. Even so, he was warmly devoted to America. "Mr. Dickinson is a very modest man, and very ingenious, as well as agreeable. He has an excellent heart, and the cause of his country lies near it," remarked Robert Treat Paine, a signer of the Declaration of Independence.

If there can be a lasting stain upon this patriot's name, it is the surprising fact that, notwithstanding his fervent opposition to English rule, he refused to sign the Declaration itself. For although he backed independence, he was convinced the time was not yet ripe for such a bold separation from England. Though his cautious stand stripped from him much of his earlier popularity, it confirmed for many his admirable strength of conviction in which it could be seen that Dickinson sought not to follow public opinion but rather to shape it.

On the morning of February 14, 1808, John Dickinson died at home at the age of 75. Warm tributes were numerous. President Jefferson and the Congress unanimously agreed to wear black armbands in honor of the statesman's memory. Fellow delegate from Delaware, George Read, left this recollection of his dear friend:

I have a vivid impression of the man, tall and spare, his hair white as snow, his face uniting with severe simplicity . . . a neatness and elegance . . . his manners a beautiful emanation of the great Christian principle of love . . . Truly he lives in my memory as the realization of my ideal of a gentleman.

5
Oliver Ellsworth
1745-1807

Chief Justice of the Supreme Court during the Presidency of John Adams, Oliver Ellsworth was born in Windsor, Connecticut, in the same year as the first chief justice, John Jay. He is also known for his Letters of a Landholder in which he skillfully endorsed ratification of the Constitution in his home state.

Graduated from Princeton College in 1766, two years before John Witherspoon became President, Ellsworth went on to become a member of the Continental Congress during the years of the Revolution. In 1787 he was chosen as a delegate to the Constitutional Convention in which he played a major role in the shaping of the national document. He did not sign the final draft, due to a sickness that forced him home early. He did, however, strongly support its ratification in Connecticut. Then, in 1789, in the formation of the new government, Ellsworth was elected as one of Connecticut's first two senators to the United States Congress. He resigned seven years later to accept his appointment to that of chief justice.

After securing a treaty of peace with France in the year 1800, the former senator and judge retired, though he continued to lend his highly-rated opinion as a member of the governor's council. He died seven years later, while still an active member of that body.

Daniel Webster, in a tribute to the worthy patriot, wrote that Ellsworth was "a gentleman who has left behind him, on the records of the government of his country, proofs of the clearest intelligence, and of the utmost purity and integrity of character."

6
Benjamin Franklin
1706-1790

In observing his vast catalog of varied accomplishments, the "American Socrates" had no equal except, perhaps, for Jefferson. And as to his influence upon the nation's character, none but Washington held greater sway. At the age of 81, Benjamin Franklin was the oldest Signer of the Constitution. Eleven years earlier, he was the oldest Signer of the Declaration of Independence. From his timeless proverbs as Poor Richard, to discovering electricity by flying his kite in a storm, Franklin was the quintessential American. He was inventor, scientist, printer, publisher, postmaster, author, diplomat, philosopher, and elder statesman all rolled into one. He was universally revered for his wit, wisdom, and creative intellect, not only in America, but in England and France as well.

When asked something of his religion by Ezra Stiles, President of Yale, Franklin replied:

Here is my creed. I believe in one God, Creator of the universe. That He governs it by His providence. That He ought to be worshipped. That the most acceptable service we render Him is doing good to His other children. That the soul of man is immortal, and will be treated with justice in another life respecting its conduct in this.

Thus we may conclude that Franklin was a man of great morals. He was . . . almost. His one self-confessed weakness is revealed in the following letter to a female neighbor:

I often pass before your house. It appears desolate to me. Formerly I broke the Commandment by coveting it along with my neighbor's wife. Now I do not covet it anymore, so I am less a sinner. But as to his wife I always find these Commandments inconvenient and I am sorry that they were ever made.

In spite of this admitted contradiction, Franklin resides in the company of America's greatest and most beloved characters.

Possibly because Franklin was generally silent as a delegate in Congress, his words were, to many, worth their weight in gold. Jefferson was one who so valued them, and linked them to another's. "I served," said he, "with General Washington in the legislature of Virginia before the Revolution, and during it with Dr. Franklin in Congress. I never heard either of them speak ten minutes at a time, nor to any but the main point which was to decide the question. They laid their shoulders to the great points, knowing that the little ones would follow of themselves." John Adams also noticed the old sage's silence, but observed it differently. He was surprised that he was appointed to the most important committees when, "from day to day (he was) sitting in silence, a great part of the time fast asleep in his chair."

Whether this was true or not, Franklin certainly resembled a jealous old father in his concern for the welfare of America, and he labored to secure it on at least three different continents. James Madison related the following anecdote at the conclusion of the Constitutional Convention:

Whilst the last members were signing, Dr. Franklin, looking towards the President's chair, at the back of which a rising sun happened to be painted, observed to a few members near him that painters have often found it difficult, in their art, to distinguish a rising from a setting sun. "I have," said he, "often and often, in the course of the session, and the vicissitude of my hopes and fears as to its issue, looked at that sun behind the president without being able to tell whether it was rising or setting; but now, at length, I have the happiness to know that it is a rising and not a setting sun."

In tribute to the venerable patriot, after his death in 1790, Jefferson proposed to Washington that he and his cabinet wear mourning. The President refused, "because he said he would not know where to draw the line if he once began that ceremony . . . I told him that the world had drawn so broad a line between him and Dr. Franklin, on the one side, and the residue of mankind, on the other, that we might wear mourning for them, and the question still remain new and undecided as to all others. He thought it best, however, to avoid it."

7
Elbridge Gerry
1744-1814

A Signer of the Declaration of Independence, Elbridge Gerry was also the fifth vice-president of the United States, and governor of Massachusetts. His early devotion to the revolutionary cause can be traced to his meeting the patriot Samuel Adams in the provincial legislature in 1772. Gerry was a nervous little man with a broad head and a long, sharp nose. "He was a respectable young merchant," wrote Benjamin Rush, "of a liberal education and considerable knowledge. He was slow in his perceptions and in his manner of doing business, and stammering in his speech, but he knew and embraced truth when he saw it." And John Adams, in his autobiography, recalled, "In this gentleman I found a faithful friend, and an ardent, persevering lover of his country, who never hesitated to promote with all his abilities and industry the boldest measures reconciled with prudence."

As his career progressed, Gerry became a somewhat controversial figure. In the Constitutional Convention of 1787, he was inconsistent and, according to another delegate, he "objected to everything he did not propose." He did not sign the final document. In a letter of explanation he wrote,

"It was painful for me, on a subject of such national importance, to differ from the respectable members who signed the Constitution. But conceiving, as I did, that the liberties of America were not secured by the system, it was my duty to oppose it."

In 1797, he was part of the trio (along with John Marshall and Charles Cotesworth Pinckney) that was sent by President Adams to negotiate a peace with France. But when he remained to continue unofficial negotiations long after his colleagues returned to America, his reputation was marred for a second time. Pinckney's deprecation was expressed in the strongest language. "I never met a man," he said, "of less candor and as much duplicity as Mr. Gerry." Adams, however, in spite of political differences, remained a lifelong friend of the merchant from Marblehead.

Although the name of Elbridge Gerry does not rank in the company of Washington and Franklin, posterity is nevertheless indebted to him for the word, "gerrymander." While Governor of Massachusetts, he signed a Bill that rearranged voting districts, thus giving political advantage to the Jeffersonian Republicans. An angry Federalist, while scanning an updated map, remarked that one district now resembled a salamander. His companion curtly replied, "No, better call it a Gerrymander."

Gerry died while serving as James Madison's vice-president at the age of 70. If, in the 42 up and down years of his public service, he did not quite find his niche, he certainly enjoyed an enviable fulfillment in his role as a husband and father. In a letter to his wife during the stormy debates of the Constitutional Convention, he wrote:

We cannot foretell or foresee the decrees of Omnipotence respecting our existence, that is a matter which He wisely conceals from mortals; but I do not expect a long life, my constitution appears not to be formed for it, and such as it is, constant attention of one kind or another prey on it; but if anything makes life in the least desirable, it is you, my dearest girl, and our lovely offspring. Detached from your comforts, life to me would be a source of evils. When troubles occur now, I reflect that they are of no consequence, compared with the happiness resulting from my little family. This opens a prospect which satisfies every desire.

8
Nathaniel Greene
1742-1786

"The man who saved the South," Nathaniel Greene was George Washington's most trustworthy general during the Revolutionary War. In the opinion of one officer, he was the greatest military genius produced during the struggle. Many years later, Thomas Jefferson remarked that the young general was "second to no one in enterprise, in resource, in sound judgment, promptitude of decision, and every other military talent." Of the fourteen generals chosen by Congress in 1775, Greene was the last, but he soon rose impressively in the judgement of the Commander-in-Chief as well as many others. His heart was fully in the battle, as apparent in a letter to Samuel Ward in the early stages of the war:

Permit me then to recommend, from the sincerity of my heart, ready at all times to bleed in my country's cause, a declaration of independence; and call upon the world, and the Great God who governs it, to witness the necessity, propriety, and rectitude thereof.

General Greene was present with Washington at Valley Forge during the bitter winter of 1777-1778. After General Gates' defeat at the battle of Camden, in 1780, Greene was given command of the Southern army. He then proceeded to push back the British and regain U.S. control in the South.

Born in Rhode Island, Greene was two inches shy of six feet, with blue-grey eyes and a ruddy complexion. He had a broad chest and shoulders with strong limbs. A vivacious temperament contributed to his bold and daring exploits as a soldier.

In his will Greene stipulated that his children should have a good education and, above all, to be taught moral values, "that best legacy of a fond father." Only three years after the treaty of Paris was signed, ending the war, Greene died at the age of 44. Another famed general, Anthony Wayne, mourned, "My dear friend General Greene is no more." Congress voted to erect a monument in honor of Greene, but it wasn't until 1877 that a bronze statue of the great Revolutionary War hero was placed in the Federal city.

9
Alexander Hamilton
1757-1804

"I consider Napoleon, Fox, and Hamilton the three greatest men of our epoch," declared the French statesman, Tallyrand, "and if I were forced to decide between the three, I would give without hesitation the first place to Hamilton." This sentiment was not unfounded, for Alexander Hamilton was, indeed, a prodigy of colossal intellect. His powers of reasoning, both military and political, were unsurpassed by the most excellent minds of his day. Yet throughout his curiously great life, he revealed a volatile temperament subject to intense emotional outbursts.

Born in the West Indies Island of Nevis, he was the illegitimate son of a mother who was dead before his teens. At the tender age of 16, he immigrated to the United States, and soon found his niche in the heated American atmosphere of the 1770s.

By the age of twenty, he had become Aide-de-Camp of General George Washington and gained the future president's unreserved confidence (though the two later had a short-lived falling out). In answer to the accusation by many that his assistant harbored an inordinate lust for personal glory, the commander-in-chief replied:

. . . *By some he is considered as an ambitious man, and therefore a dangerous one. That he is ambitious, I shall readily grant, but it is of that laudable kind, which prompts a man to excel in whatever he takes in hand. He is enterprising, quick in his perceptions, and his judgment intuitively great; qualities essential to a military character.*

Awkward in appearance, with closely set blue eyes, and a nose of conspicuous length, he admitted, "I am not handsome." Nevertheless, his face was remarkably expressive, his smile extraordinarily sweet, and he seemed to possess that rare quality of charisma with which few are gifted.

Chosen as Washington's secretary of the treasury in the nation's first administration, Hamilton exhibited his superior talents in leading the country through its early financial crises. In spite of his obvious genius, he soon was at bitter odds with another genius, Thomas Jefferson, Washington's secretary of state. While Hamilton wished to concentrate the power of the federal government, Jefferson strove to delegate much of it to the individual states. These two great statesmen forged the new Republic's two great political parties; Hamilton led the Federalists, and Jefferson, the Democratic-Republicans.

In spite of gaining lasting fame as one of the greatest of the Founding Fathers, Alexander Hamilton was a frustrated and discontented man during his own lifetime. In 1802, he lamented that

Mine is an odd destiny. Perhaps no man in the United States has sacrificed or done more for the present constitution than myself; and contrary to all my anticipations of its fate . . . I am still laboring to prop the frail and worthless fabric, yet I have the murmurs of its friends no less than the curses of its foes for my reward. What can I do better than withdraw from the scene? Every day proves to me more and more that the American world was not made for me.

Two years later, in a duel with his avowed enemy, Aaron Burr, a man even more ambitious than himself, Hamilton was mortally wounded and universally mourned. "It is known," said a contemporary, "what a thrill of horror, what a sharp, terrible pang ran through the nation, proving the comprehension by the entire people of what was lost, when Aaron Burr took from his country and the world that important life. In the most distant extremities of the Union men felt that one of the first intellects of the age had been extinguished."

10
John Hancock
1737-1793

"There, I think King George can read that!" exclaimed the president of Congress as he lifted his pen from his oversized signature on the Declaration of Independence. John Hancock was a great patriot and a vain man. Bold in his denunciation of British authority over the colonies, he was just as fervent in his desire for the praise of his fellow countrymen, which, with good cause, they loved to give the effervescent statesman. He was one of the wealthiest men in Boston and sought to use that wealth to further the revolutionary cause. Hancock was an extremely handsome man and always dressed most impressively. He was nearly six feet tall, though he stooped a little as he grew older. His health was not very good, often being confined to his bed due to the gout.

In the several years preceding the revolutionary war, Hancock became one of the leading figures in the growing resistance to British rule in America. He was widely admired for his fearless stand against the king in behalf of the freedom-loving colonists, particularly in the besieged town of Boston. It was here in 1773 that the notorious "Boston Tea Party" occurred. Hancock was in cahoots with this risky venture but was far too well known to the British authorities to take part as one of the "Indians," though a certain George Hewes thought he noticed delicate ruffles sticking out from under one of his fellow Indian's disguises. And not only so, but he heard from the same a grunt and a "me know you," which resembled Hancock's voice. Indeed, he was, according to John Adams, an "essential character" in this great American crisis.

It is Adams who reveals the not-so-admirable side of Hancock (though it is somewhat humorous) in the following narrative:

When Congress had assembled, I rose in my place . . . with a motion, in form, that Congress would adopt the army at Cambridge, and appoint a General . . . I had no hesitation to declare that I had but one gentleman in my mind for that important command, and that was a gentleman from Virginia who was among us and very well known to all of us, a gentleman whose skill and experience as an officer, whose independent fortune, great talents, and excellent universal character would command the approbation of all America . . .

Mr. Washington, who happened to sit near the door, as soon as he heard me allude to him, from his usual modesty darted into the library-room. Mr. Hancock—who was our President, which gave me an opportunity to observe his countenance while I was speaking on the state of the Colonies, the army at Cambridge, and the enemy—heard me with visible pleasure: but when I came to describe Washington for the commander, I never remarked a more sudden and striking change of countenance. Mortification and resentment were expressed as forcibly as his face could exhibit them. Mr. Samuel Adams seconded the motion, and that did not soften the President's physiognomy at all.

In 1780, Hancock was elected to be the first state governor of Massachusetts. He served in this post until 1785, when he was elected again after a ten year interval to be president of Congress. In 1787 he resumed the governorship of Massachusetts, which he held until his death in 1793.

Uncharacteristically, Hancock had asked to be buried without public display. Nevertheless, at his death on October 8, a witness recorded that ". . . there were upwards of 20,000 people in the procession. And the spectators—every house and street was thronged." During his life, John Hancock craved the approbation of his peers and, indeed, he earned it. But, ironically, it was at his funeral, where ". . . the most solemn silence and attention pervaded every rank of the multitude," that he received the greater tribute, which he could never enjoy.

11
Patrick Henry
1736-1799

Several times governor of Virginia during and after the Revolution, Patrick Henry was considered by many to be premature in his revolutionary fervor. The passing of two hundred years has proven that he was a step ahead of his time—"He left all of us far behind," remarked Jefferson fifty years later.

Henry is best known for his impassioned speech before the Virginia Provincial Convention in which he declared, "Give me liberty, or give me death!" One of those present at the time remarked that Henry's "voice, countenance, and gestures gave an irresistible force to his words, which no description could make intelligible to one who had never seen him, nor heard him speak." Another gave this account:

Henry arose with an unearthly fire burning in his eye. He commenced somewhat calmly—but the smothered excitement began to play more and more upon his features, and thrill in the tones of his voice . . . Finally his pale face and glaring eyes became terrible to look upon. Men leaned forward in their seats with their heads strained forward, their faces pale and their eyes glaring like the speaker's. His last exclamation—"Give me liberty, or give me death"—was like the shout of the leader who turns back the rout of battle. When he sat down, I felt sick with excitement. Every eye yet gazed entranced on Henry. It seemed as if a word from him would have led to any wild explosion of violence. Men looked beside themselves.

Henry was not a handsome man and was somewhat bald, always wearing a wig in public. His features were very distinct with blue eyes and a countenance that was both intelligent and animated. Judge Spencer Roane describes his disposition:

I am positive that I never saw him in a passion, nor apparently even out of temper. Circumstances which would have highly irritated other men had no such visible effect on him. He was always calm and collected, and the rude attacks of his adversaries in debate only whetted the poignancy of his satire.

And in 1818, John Adams wrote of his friend:

From personal acquaintance, perhaps I might say a friendship, with Mr. Henry of more than thirty years, and from all that I have heard or read of him, I have always considered him a gentleman of deep reflection, keen sagacity, clear foresight, daring enterprise, inflexible intrepidity, and untainted integrity, with an ardent zeal for the liberties, the honor, and the felicity of his country and his species.

Although Henry was obviously in support of independence, he was not present at the signing of the historic declaration, due to his extensive involvement in Virginia politics. Nor did he affix his signature to the Constitution. The reason in this case was a strong opposition to it. His fear was that it gave too much power to the federal government, thus putting at risk the sovereign rights of the individual states. Along with George Mason, a fellow Virginian, he fought fiercely against its ratification in his home state. He lost the battle, and with it, his prominence in national politics. Nevertheless, he was so universally esteemed as a statesman and orator, that President Washington offered him the post of secretary of state in his cabinet, as well as that of chief justice of the Supreme Court. He refused both.

Patrick Henry died only six months before the retired Washington, in the presence of his sorrowing family. "Oh, how wretched should I be at this moment," he declared, "if I had not made my peace with God!"

12
Stephen Hopkins
1707-1785

Nine times elected colonial governor of Rhode Island, Stephen Hopkins was a signer of the Declaration of Independence. He was also chief justice of the superior court previous to and after his tenure as governor. He was a venerable man, according to a fellow delegate to the Second Continental Congress, "of an original understanding, extensive reading, and great integrity."

Hopkins was fervent in his devotion to the revolutionary effort. On the night of April 19, 1775, when news reached Providence that British troops had fired that morning upon minutemen at Lexington Commons, he immediately sent this report:

To Major General Potter:

This evening intelligence hath been received that about twelve hundred of the Regulars have proceeded from Boston towards Concord, and having fired upon and killed a number of the inhabitants of Lexington, are now actually engaged in butchering and destroying our brethren there in the most inhuman manner, that the inhabitants oppose them with zeal and courage and numbers have already fallen on both sides. Reinforcements were at ten o'clock under motion from Boston, and the Provincials were alarmed and mustering as fast as possible. It appears necessary therefore that we immediately make some provision for their assistance . . .

The country's friend and yours,
S. Hopkins

Being one of the oldest members of the Continental Congress (He was only a year younger than his close friend Mr. Franklin of Philadelphia.), and respected both for his acquired knowledge and mature understanding, Hopkins was an invaluable contributor to the American cause until his death at the age of 78. John Adams, a member with him on the committee to establish a navy, wrote the following account of his partner's utility in labor as well as in leisure:

> . . . *the pleasantest part of my labors for the four years I spent in Congress from 1774 to 1778 were in this naval committee. Mr. Lee, Mr. Gadsden were sensible men, and very cheerful, but Governor Hopkins of Rhode Island, about seventy years of age, kept us all alive. Upon business, his experience and judgment were very useful. But when the business of the evening was over, he kept us in conversation till eleven, and sometimes twelve o'clock. His custom was to drink nothing all day, nor till eight o'clock in the evening, and then his beverage was Jamaica spirit and water. It gave him wit, humor, anecdotes, science and learning. He had read Greek, Roman and British history, and was familiar with English poetry, particularly Pope, Thomson and Milton, and the flow of his soul made all his reading our own and seemed to bring to recollection in all of us all we had ever read. I could neither eat nor drink in these days. The other gentlemen were very temperate. Hopkins never drank to excess, but all he drank was immediately not only converted into wit, sense, knowledge and good humor, but inspired us with similar qualities.*

13
John Jay
1745-1829

First chief justice of the Supreme Court, John Jay was a man whose greatness was paradoxical. Beneath a stoic composure, he possessed an intense passion to know the truth, and then to pursue it despite any personal loss. He was perfectly content, having done his duty, to receive praise or condemnation. Not one to accept the popularly held tenets of his day without first searching out the matter himself, he once wrote a minister:

In forming and settling my belief relative to the doctrines of Christianity, I adopted no articles from creeds, but such only as, on careful examination, I found to be confirmed by the Bible.

In appearance, Jay was just under six feet tall and rather thin. His face was pale but amiable in expression, with penetrating, dark blue eyes. He tended to lean forward when standing or walking—likely the result of sitting at his desk for hours at a time, poring over his books.

Jay served a term as president of Congress during the Revolutionary War, during which time he worked for the adoption of the Declaration of Independence. Besides co-writing that brilliant defense of the Constitution, The *Federalist Papers,* he also wrote the treaty bearing his name, which the United States made with Great Britain in 1794. Then, in 1795, he became governor of New York and remained in that position for six years.

But perhaps his greatest legacy has already been mentioned—that of being the first chief justice of the Supreme Court. President Washington had such high regard for Jay's impeccable character that he offered him his choice of positions in the new administration. That of chief justice was chosen, as it seemed the office in which he could best support and defend the untested

Constitution. His jealousy over it was understandable, for, "That gentleman," wrote John Adams, "had as much influence in the preparatory measures in digesting the Constitution, and obtaining its adoption, as any man in the nation."

In the closing months of his useful life, Jay was no longer able to walk by himself. He spent much time with his children, his wife having died almost thirty years earlier, listening to books being read aloud. Although he could not attend church, he often had the Lord's Supper in his own home. In his will, he directed that his funeral be managed frugally, and "instead thereof I give two hundred dollars to any one poor deserving widow or orphan of this town, whom my children shall select." John Jay died on the night of May 14, 1829. In a brief eulogy, another chief justice remembered the worthy statesman:

Few men in any country, perhaps scarce one in this, have filled a larger space, and few ever passed through life with such perfect purity, integrity, and honour.

14
Thomas Jefferson
1743-1826

"I have sworn on the altar of God eternal hostility against every form of tyranny over the mind of man." So said the author of the Declaration of Independence and the third president of the United States, revealing his life-long passion for liberty. For many, Thomas Jefferson is the embodiment of the American spirit of freedom. He firmly believed that the common man exercising his natural rights to "life, liberty and the pursuit of happiness," was the cornerstone of American greatness. During his highly prolific career, he was recognized as a man of many abilities: president, statesman, writer, philosopher, musician, architect, scientist, and inventor. "He possessed a genius of the first order," wrote Benjamin Rush, "It was universal in its objects. He was not less distinguished for his political than his mathematical and philosophical knowledge." In appearance, he was slender and well over six feet tall, with reddish hair. He tended to be rather informal and was, in fact, the first president to have his guests shake his hand rather than follow the formal custom of bowing.

In the spring of 1776, Jefferson wrote the Declaration of Independence, in which he stated that men are created free by God, and are morally bound to shake off the yoke of a despotic government. He served as governor of Virginia for two terms during the Revolutionary War. Afterwards, in 1785, he was appointed in Benjamin Franklin's stead as Minister to France. There he was asked, "It is you, Sir, who replace Franklin?" "No Sir," replied Jefferson, "I succeed him; no one can replace him."

Upon his return to America in 1789, Jefferson was appointed by newly elected President Washington to be his secretary of state. Thus began an ever-increasing polarization of political philosophy between himself and the secretary of the treasury, Alexander Hamilton. It was this division that was the beginning of parties in American politics. Jefferson resigned from Washington's Cabinet after his first term.

In the election of 1800, there was a tie between Jefferson and Aaron Burr. The House of Representatives was to break the tie. Ironically, it was Jefferson's old nemesis, Hamilton, whose influence gave him the presidency. Though they were still at odds, Hamilton thought Burr the more dangerous of the two.

Following George Washington's precedent, Jefferson refused to run for a third term. He gave his support to his secretary of state, James Madison. "Never did a prisoner released from his chains," he wrote, "feel such relief as I shall on shaking off the shackles of power." He retired at last from public life at the age of 65 to enjoy his varied intellectual pursuits as well as answering an increasing demand for correspondence from friends across the country. Presidents Madison and Monroe were among those seeking advice from their old mentor, the Sage of Monticello.

"I always loved Jefferson, and still love him," said John Adams in 1811. Thus were two of America's greatest sons reconciled in their interrupted friendship, which they now enjoyed until their death on the same day, July 4, 1826, exactly fifty years after the Declaration of Independence.

15
Richard Henry Lee
1732-1794

RESOLVED, That these United Colonies are, and of right ought to be, free and independent States, that they are absolved from all allegiance to the British Crown, and that all political connection between them and the State of Great Britain is, and ought to be totally dissolved.

On June 7, 1776, Richard Henry Lee submitted this celebrated resolution to the Continental Congress, and in so doing, lit the spark that burst into flames less than a month later.

Tall and thin with sharp, well-defined features, Lee was born thirty-three days before, and five miles away from, George Washington in Westmoreland County, Virginia. He had three brothers who were prominent as well in the era; Arthur, William, and Francis Lightfoot. Richard Henry was the twelfth president of Congress as well as one of Virginia's first U.S. senators. He was the most prominent of the Virginia delegates leading up to the Declaration, Jefferson being only 32 years old at the time. He was recognized as an exceptional orator and had thereby gained the title Cicero by his colleagues. Nevertheless, he lacked the emotional heat so often felt in the fiery speeches of those days.

In the debates over ratification of the Constitution, Lee was a strong voice for the Anti-federalists in Virginia, along with Patrick Henry, George Mason, and others. Their argument was that the new government would be entrusted with too much power, by which it would remove itself from the active participation of the people. Lee's contribution, in particular, was his Letters of a Federal Farmer, which became a source book for the dissenters.

At the age of sixty, Lee resigned from the Senate because of his failing health. Two years later, in 1794, he died at his home, "Chantilly."

16
James Madison
1751-1836

Known as the "Father of the Constitution," Madison played a central and authoritative role in the debates that led up to the final draft of the United States Constitution. While his speaking ability was not that of a John Adams or a Patrick Henry, his genius for calm, quiet logic made a place for him among the greatest of the founding fathers. Though small and frail in body, the stature of his mind was monumental, being thoroughly acquainted with political theory and the history of the nations. As well as greatness of mind, the fourth president also had a good conscience. John Witherspoon, president of Princeton University, recalled "that he never knew him do or say an improper thing" while a student.

During the Constitutional Convention in the summer of 1787, Madison expressed concern with the weakness and insufficiency of the Articles of Confederation, and strove for a stronger central government. He took notes on the daily debates, which remain as the only full report of the arguments and compromises that took place within those secret meetings. He also led the proceedings with such a comprehensive understanding, that William Pierce of Georgia was led to write,

Every person seems to acknowledge his greatness. He blends together the profound politician with the scholar. In the management of every great question he evidently takes the lead.

After signing the Constitution, Madison went to work, along with Alexander Hamilton and John Jay, in defending it in a series of powerful articles known as The *Federalist Papers*. Serving in the House of Representatives during the Washington administration, Madison proved to be one of its ablest members. He was responsible for the drafting of the first ten amendments to the Constitution, known as the Bill of Rights. He also proposed the establishment of the Departments of State, Treasury, and War. Although he voiced the Federalists' argument for greater federal power, he stopped short of Hamilton's policies for an extensive federal rule. He became increasingly supportive of the Anti-Federalist view, which favored individual state sovereignty in all but national matters.

When President Washington offered him the post of secretary of state in 1794, Madison declined, but seven years later, he accepted the same appointment by newly elected President Jefferson. He held this post for eight years until he himself was elected to the presidency in 1809. The War of 1812 revealed a president who, though a brilliant statesman, was sorely lacking the administrative powers needed for such a time. His wife, Dolly, however, brought a charm and a cheer to the White House that made her one of the most beloved First Ladies of all time. He was succeeded as president in 1817 by his secretary of state, James Monroe, the last of the "Virginia Dynasty" of Jefferson, Madison, and Monroe.

Having served his country for more that four decades, Madison retired at the age of sixty-five to his home in Montpelier, Virginia. For two more decades, he lived peacefully with his wife until his death on June 28th, 1836, having been the last surviving signer of the Constitution of which he was the Father.

17
George Mason
1725-1792

George Mason was author of the Virginia Declaration of Rights, which begins, "That all men are by nature equally free and independent and have certain inherent rights . . . namely, the enjoyment of life and liberty . . . and pursuing and obtaining happiness and safety." This was a model for Jefferson's drafting of the Declaration of Independence. James Madison drew from the document as well in his work on the Bill of Rights.

A member of the Constitutional Convention of 1787, Mason greatly contributed to the debates that led to the writing of the Constitution. He refused, in the end, to sign the final draft because it contained no bill of rights and did not provide for the termination of slavery. In so doing, he alienated himself from many of his colleagues and close friends, one of which was George Washington. Mason explains his motives in the following account:

You know the friendship which has long existed (indeed from our early youth) between General Washington and myself. I believe there are few men in whom he placed greater confidence; but it is possible my opposition to the new government . . . may have altered the case. In this important trust, I am truly conscious of having acted from the purest motives of honesty, and love to my country . . . and I would not forfeit the approbation of my own mind for the approbation of any man or all the men upon earth. My conduct as a public man, through the whole of the late glorious Revolution, has been such as, I trust, will administer comfort to me in those moments when I shall most want it, and smooth the bed of death.

After the Convention, Mason worked with Patrick Henry in opposing ratification in Virginia. Although he lost the esteem of several contemporaries because of his obstinacy, the fact remains that a bill of rights was, indeed, written, and that slavery was eventually abolished.

Mason was an extremely private man. Declining to serve in many offices that were offered to him, he cherished the peace and quiet that could only be had apart from public life. In his will, he advised his sons to refrain from a life of politics unless they could not be happy otherwise. Nevertheless, realizing the historical significance of that in which he had taken part, he remarked, "Taking a retrospective view of what is passed, we seem to have been treading upon enchanted ground." He died at his beloved home, Gunston Hall, in 1792, during Washington's presidency. Almost thirty years after Mason's death, in 1821, Jefferson wrote:

He was a man of the first order of wisdom among those who acted on the theatre of the revolution, of expansive mind, profound judgment, cogent in argument, learned in the lore of our former Constitution (Articles of Confederation) . . . His elocution was neither flowing nor smooth; but his language was strong, his manner most impressive and strengthened by a dash of biting cynicism when provocation made it seasonable.

18
Thomas Paine
1737-1809

"These are the times that try men's souls,'" wrote the man who, perhaps more than any other, turned public opinion strongly in favor of a declaration for independence. Indeed, the Declaration was adopted less than six months after his best-selling pamphlet, *Common Sense,* was published. Thomas Paine was unsurpassed in his ability to express the American spirit of freedom and independence with such a passionate understanding. George Washington wrote that, "the sound doctrine and unanswerable reasoning contained in the pamphlet Common Sense will not leave numbers at a loss to decide upon the propriety of separation." And John Adams offered this tribute: "History is to ascribe the Revolution to Thomas Paine."

An Englishman who met Ben Franklin in London, Paine was convinced by the diplomat that he should move to America, which he did in 1774. Shortly after his arrival, Dr. Benjamin Rush persuaded him to write the aforementioned *Common Sense.* He then enlisted in the army as an aide to General Nathaniel Greene. While the Continental forces were at their low point, and public opinion of the war was shaky, Paine once again took up his pen and wrote *The Crisis,* in which he stated:

Tyranny, like hell is not easily conquered; yet we have this consolation with us, that the harder the conflict, the more glorious the triumph. What we obtain too cheap, we esteem too lightly: it is dearness only that gives everything its value.

It cannot be challenged that Paine, as a writer, was invaluable to the Revolutionary Cause. Thomas Edison complained, "What a pity these works are not today the schoolbooks for all children!" But the opinions of Paine, as a man, are as disparate as the divide between Washington and Arnold. Theodore Roosevelt described him as a "filthy little atheist," while Edison said, "I have always regarded Paine as one of the greatest of all Americans."

Standing at five feet, nine inches tall, Paine was slender with brilliant blue eyes and a prominent nose. In spite of his success as a writer, he lived most of his life on the verge of poverty, being prone to give away much of his money. He never cursed, and greatly disliked obscene stories. He loved children, but easily made men his enemies by expressing his opinions in the most forcible and argumentative manner. He was not an atheist, as Roosevelt charged, for he believed in God, and heartily endorsed the system of morality instituted by Jesus Christ. Nevertheless, he did see as irrational the Christian doctrine of the divinity of Christ and went to great lengths to explain why in his later work, *The Age of Reason,* which he wrote from a French prison.

Paine returned to the United States in 1802 and lived in New York until his death seven years later. Although he had done great things for his adopted country, he died in a run-down boarding house and was, for the most part, unmourned. An admirer by the name of William Cobbett determined to take Paine's body to England and set up a shrine there in his honor. One night he secretly dug up the coffin and escaped with it. Through several exchanges, however, the corpse was lost, and to this day Thomas Paine has no grave.

19
Charles Cotesworth Pinckney
1746-1825

Defeated in his presidential bids of 1804 and 1808, Charles Cotesworth Pinckney was nevertheless a patriot of eminent service in the Revolution, as well a positive force in the early decades of the Union. He was a signer of the Constitution, although he is probably best known for his famous reply, "Millions for defense, but not a cent for tribute!" (his actual words were, "No! No! Not a sixpence!" but were altered to produce the more poetic slogan), when the French offered to keep peace with America for a large sum of money in the XYZ Affair. When Charles was only six years old, his father wrote in his will,

And to the end that my beloved son Charles Cotesworth may the better be enabled to become the head of his family, and prove not only of service and advantage to his country, but also an honour to his stock and kindred, my order and direction is that my said son be virtuously, religiously and liberally brought up so . . . that he will employ all his future abilities in the service of God and his country, in the cause of virtuous liberty, as well religious as civil, and in support of private right and justice between man and man.

Some 23 years later, the stout, round- faced Pinckney risked both his wealth and status as an influential South Carolina plantation owner when he entered the Continental Army. He served as an aide to General Washington at the battles of Brandywine and Germantown in 1777. When the British captured Charleston in 1780, he was taken captive for nearly two years. To a British major, he wrote, "I entered into this cause after reflection and through principle. My heart is altogether American, and neither severity, nor favor, nor poverty, nor affluence can ever induce me to swerve from it." And to another officer: "The freedom and independence of my country are the gods of my idolatry." By war's end, he had attained the rank of brigadier general.

That Pinckney put the interests of his country before his own is revealed in an episode involving Alexander Hamilton and Henry Knox. When George Washington was called out of retirement by President Adams in light of the threat of war with France, the aging general was perplexed as to how he should order the three officers' ranking. While Hamilton threatened, and Knox sulked, Pinckney was content to receive his appointment as an honor and privilege. When Washington let it be known that the order would be Hamilton, Pinckney, and Knox, the southern general cheerfully took his place under Hamilton, and even offered to give Knox the second position if it would soothe his wounded feelings. Secretary of State, Timothy Pickering, wondered at Pinckney's benevolence, calling him "truly a patriot and an honest man." Washington himself agreed, having several years earlier written, "In this gentleman many valuable qualities are to be found—he is of unquestionable bravery—is a man of strict honor, erudition and good sense."

After months of declining health at the age of eighty, Charles Cotesworth Pinckney died on August 16, 1825. William Drayton recalled his "rare felicity of running an unbroken career of virtue and usefulness — honored and honorable from the bloom of youth to the maturity of manhood and the frosts of old age." In the churchyard of St. Michael's in Charleston, his tombstone reads:

To the memory of General Charles Cotesworth Pinckney, one of the founders of the American Republic. In war he was the companion in arms, and the friend of Washington. In peace he enjoyed his unchanging confidence and maintained with enlightened zeal the principles of his administration and of the constitution. As a statesman he bequeathed to his country the sentiment, Millions for defense, not a cent for tribute. As a lawyer, his learning was various and profound, his principles pure, his practice liberal. With all the accomplishments of the Gentleman, he combined the virtues of the Patriot and the piety of the Christian. His name is recorded in the history of his country, inscribed on the charter of her liberties, and cherished in the affections of her citizens.

20
William Prescott
1726-1795

William Prescott was one of the heroes at the Battle of Bunker Hill, where he uttered his now famous command, "Don't fire until you see the whites of their eyes! Then aim at their waistbands; and be sure to pick off the commanders, known by their handsome coats."

A soldier in his teens, Prescott fought for England, as did many pre-revolutionary figures, in the French and Indian War. A colonel at the outbreak of the Revolutionary War, he rushed with his men to Concord as soon as he received word of the British offensive. He did not, however, arrive in time to help the embattled minutemen. It was his cousin, Dr. Samuel Prescott, who had brought warning of the approaching British to the town when Paul Revere had been captured in Lexington.

Two months later, at Bunker Hill, he oversaw the hurried digging of trenches the night before the British attacked. In the morning, he commanded the militia in successfully repelling the enemy twice until his men ran out of ammunition and had to retreat at last. He relates the details in a letter to John Adams:

. . . On the 16th June, in the evening, I received orders to march to Breed's Hill in Charlestown, with a party of about one thousand men . . . We arrived at the spot, the lines were drawn by the engineer, and we began the entrenchment about twelve o'clock; and plying the work with all possible expedition till just before sunrising, when the enemy began a very heavy cannonading and bombardment . . .

. . . About an hour after the enemy landed, they began to march to the attack in three columns. I commanded my Lieutenant-Col. Robinson and Major Woods, each with a detachment, to flank the enemy, who, I have reason to think, behaved with prudence and courage. I was now left with perhaps one hundred and fifty men in the fort. The enemy advanced and

fired very hotly on the fort, and meeting with a warm reception, there was a very smart firing on both sides. After a considerable time, finding our ammunition was almost spent, I commanded a cessation till the enemy advanced within thirty yards, when we gave them such a hot fire that they were obliged to retire nearly one hundred and fifty yards before they could rally and come up again to the attack.

Our ammunition being nearly exhausted, we could keep up only a scattering fire. The enemy, being numerous, surrounded our little fort, began to mount our lines and enter the fort with their bayonets. We were obliged to retreat through them, while they kept up as hot a fire at it was possible for them to make. We, having very few bayonets, could make no resistance. We kept the fort about one hour and twenty minutes after the attack with small arms . . .

Technically, the battle was a British victory. The numbers, however, tell another story. Out of 2,500 men, the British lost about 1,150. The Americans lost only 400 men out of around 1,600. "A dear bought victory," lamented British General, Sir Henry Clinton, "Another such would have ruined us." And General Gage, complained that "the loss we have sustained is greater than we can bear." He was removed from his command four months later. Of Colonel Prescott, Daniel Webster later remarked, "From the first breaking of the ground to the retreat, he acted the most important part; and if it were proper to give the battle a name, from any distinguished agent in it, it should be called Prescott's battle."

21
Paul Revere
1735-1818

The double dealing Hypocrite,
I try to shun, with all my might,
The Knave, I hate; the Cheat despise;
The Flatterer fly; but court the Wise.

Thus wrote a simple man who typified the American ideals of industry and patriotism. Paul Revere was no Madison, whose knowledge of political history was colossal, nor a Jefferson, whose mind seemed to comprehend the loftiest philosophies. He was not one to indulge in theory when he could lay his hands on a task, and simply do it.

The stocky, dark-eyed Revere was a silversmith, whose works are now regarded as masterpieces. He was also a dentist, who, after the Battle of Bunker Hill, identified the fallen hero, Doctor Joseph Warren, by the gold teeth he had set in his mouth. He cast cannons and bullets during the Revolutionary War, and afterward, bells. He was the first man in the United States to roll copper into sheets, which was used in the building of much needed ships. He was skilled as well in the art of copper-plate engraving.

In spite of these notable enterprises, Revere has lasting fame as a true American patriot. He was an integral member of the Sons of Liberty, and close friends with John Hancock and Samuel Adams. He was one of the "Mohawks" in the Boston Tea Party of 1773. And on the night of April 18, 1775, he rode his horse into immortality as the "Midnight Rider" who warned the colonists of the approaching British troops.

When he died at the age of 83, Paul Revere was destined to become one of America's greatest legendary heroes. But the unassuming Bostonian was honored in this excerpt from the Boston Intelligencer in 1818:

Cool in thought, ardent in action, he was well adapted to form plans, and to carry them into execution — both for the benefit of himself and the service of others. In the early scenes of our revolutionary drama, which were laid in this metropolis as well as at a later period of its progress, his country found him one of the most zealous and active of her sons.

22
Benjamin Rush
1746-1813

The leading physician of his era, Benjamin Rush has been called the father of American medicine. He signed the Declaration of Independence and was surgeon general of the Continental Army. His personality was marked with dignity, charisma, and a quick intelligence. While quite amiable, he was a serious man, and the sound of laughter was seldom heard from his lips. Of medium height, with a slender but masculine form, the doctor had a high and broad forehead and piercing blue eyes.

Rush was very opinionated and subject to occasional indiscretions. "Oh, for a Moses or a Joshua to deliver his people!" he once wrote to Patrick Henry during the Revolutionary War. In the letter, he sharply criticized General Washington's actions as below that of a great military character. The general somehow came into possession of the letter, and it was ever after one of the doctor's greatest regrets.

One of Rush's greatest pleasures, however, was to mediate the reconciliation of two estranged friends, Thomas Jefferson and John Adams, whom he called the North and South poles of the American Revolution. To Jefferson he wrote in 1811:

> . . . I consider your early attachment to Mr. Adams, and his to you . . . I consider how much the liberties and independence of the United States owe to the concert of your principles and labors . . . Posterity will revere the friendship of two ex-Presidents that were once opposed to each other. Human nature will be a gainer by it.

Friends again throughout the rest of their lives, the two statesmen received word of Rush's death only two years after the above letter. "Another of our friends of seventy-six is gone, my dear Sir," wrote Jefferson to

Adams, "another of the co-signers of the Independence of our country. And a better man than Rush could not have left us, more benevolent, more learned, of finer genius, or more honest." Adams mourned as well:

As a man of science, letters, taste, sense, philosophy, patriotism, religion, morality, merit, usefulness, taken altogether Rush has not left his equal in America, nor that I know in the world. In him is taken away, and in a manner most sudden and totally unexpected, a main prop of my life.

But the ex-president had no regrets, having eight years earlier written his old friend, "It seemeth unto me, that you and I ought not to die without saying Goodbye or bidding each other Adieu."

Benjamin Rush died on April 19, 1813, the 38th anniversary of the first shots of the Revolutionary War. The bronze plaque at his grave acknowledges his universal fame:

Benjamin Rush
1746-1813
Father of American Psychiatry
Signer of the Declaration of Independence
Heroic Physician, Teacher, Humanitarian
Physician General of the Continental Army
Physician to the Pennsylvania Hospital
Professor of Physic, University of Pennsylvania

23
Melancton Smith
1744-1798

A wealthy lawyer and merchant from New York, Melancton Smith was a delegate in the Continental Congress during the years 1785-1788. One of the Antifederalist's most effective speakers, Smith also served in his state's first provincial Congress in 1775, where, as captain of the Rangers, he was instrumental in forming regiments of militia men at the outbreak of the Revolutionary War.

The son of Samuel and Elizabeth Smith, Melancton was schooled at home. He became a landowner at an early age due to his diligent labors at a local retail store. He quickly earned a reputation for being well-read, honest, and a youth of extraordinary ability. In his personal life, Smith was a deeply religious man. He was intimately involved with the organization of the Washington Hollow Presbyterian Church. One who knew him well said he was "as pure a man as ever lived."

In 1782, General Washington appointed him to a commission to settle disputes between the army and its contractors at West Point and other vital stations.

The year 1788 was a crucial one in the national debate over the federal Constitution. Smith played a central role in the Poughkeepsie Convention, where he brilliantly defended the Antifederalist cause. He skillfully engaged in a contest of words with the more prominent Alexander Hamilton, who was a staunch supporter of the document. Smith protested that the government, under this system, "will fall into the hands of the few and the great." His antagonism, like that of George Mason and others, was fomented by the absence of a bill of rights in the final draft. He warned that, "this will be a government of oppression." When asked if he might change his mind, he replied, "If my sentiments are altered, it is to think it worse." Nevertheless, when it became apparent that the opposition could not prevail, he joined in support of the measure. It was this action that divided much of the Antifederalist force and brought Smith into disrepute among many of his colleagues, including Governor George Clinton.

In 1798, Melancton Smith was an early victim of the Yellow Fever epidemic in New York City. Although his name remains for the most part unrecognized, he was known by many in his day as "one of the ablest debaters in the country."

24
Joseph Warren
1741-1775

"Those fellows say we won't fight; By heavens, I hope I shall die up to my knees in blood!" Thus prophesied one of America's dearest defenders, and the first great martyr of the Revolutionary War, Joseph Warren. Soon after, at the tender age of thirty-four, he was cut down by British gunshot in the Battle of Bunker Hill.

A wealthy Boston physician of noticeable status, Warren was a leader, along with Sam Adams and others, in the Sons of Liberty. The doctor was a highly spirited youth, fully engaged in the cause of freedom. Had he lived, he surely would have ranked in company with the greatest soldiers and statesmen of the Revolutionary period.

The famous "Midnight Ride" of Paul Revere began under the instructions of Warren, being at the time president of the provincial revolutionary congress. He was also one of the planners of the Boston Tea Party only two years earlier. After chasing the British back to Boston from Concord, he was appointed to command the Massachusetts militia. Against the urging of his peers, he insisted in fighting at Bunker Hill as a private volunteer, on the front lines, rather than as an officer. It was here, under William Prescott's command, that the beloved patriot fell.

British General William Howe, who led the redcoat's charge, remarked upon the discovery of his body that Warren's death was worth that of five hundred American privates. One loyalist gloated over the tragedy, "Since Adams went to Philadelphia, one Warren, a rascally patriot and apothecary of this town, has had the lead in the Provincial Congress. He signed commissions and acted as president. This fellow happily was killed, in coming out of the trenches the other day, where he had commanded and spirited the people to defend the lines."

But Abigail Adams, writing to her husband, John, expressed it in different terms altogether:

> *Not all the havoc and devastation (the British) have made has wounded me like the death of Warren. We want him in the Senate; we want him in his profession; we want him in the field. We mourn for the citizen, the senator, the physician, and the warrior. May we have others raised up in his room.*

25
George Washington
1732-1799

"I have no wish superior to that of promoting the happiness and welfare of this country." So said the man who has come to be known as the "Father of His Country." George Washington was a man whom destiny, it seems, took hold of and thrust into greatness. And into that greatness he brought his country. "Light Horse Harry" Lee, father of Confederate General, Robert E. Lee, was Washington's friend and one of his officers in the War for Independence. He gave this portrait of the American hero: "Possessing a clear and penetrating mind, a strong and sound judgment, calmness and temper for deliberation, with invincible firmness and perseverance in resolutions maturely formed, drawing from all, acting from himself, with incorruptible integrity and unvarying patriotism, his own superiority and the public confidence alike marked him as the man designed by Heaven to lead in the great political, as well as military, events, which have distinguished the area of his life. The finger of an overruling Providence pointing at Washington was neither mistaken nor unobserved."

In appearance, the General was striking and impressive, and unlike anyone else, with a lofty and commanding stature. In his prime, he was six feet, two inches tall and weighed about two hundred and ten pounds. His strength was unusually great. His limbs were large and long. Lafayette, speaking to Washington's stepson some 25 years after his death, said, "I never saw so large a hand on any human being, as the general's. You were a very little gentleman, with a feather in your hat, and holding fast to one finger of the good general's remarkable hand, which was all you could do, my dear sir, at that time."

During an episode in the French and Indian War, Washington avoided an almost certain death while he was an aide to the British General, Edward Braddock, on a campaign to drive out the French from disputed lands. When the French and Indians attacked the unprepared British troops, Braddock was mortally wounded in the confusion. With men falling on either side, and two horses shot out from under him, Washington's calm and efficient leadership saved many lives in the retreat. For this courageous feat, Washington was raised to the rank of colonel as well as having gained a reputation as an able leader. Years later, an Indian Chief related the following:

I am a chief, and the ruler over many tribes. My influence extends to the waters of the great lakes, and to the far blue mountains. I have travelled a long and weary path, that I might see the young warrior of the great battle. It was on the day, when the white man's blood, mixed with the streams of our forest, that I first beheld this chief; I called to my young men and said, mark yon tall and daring warrior? He is not of the red coat tribe—he hath an Indian's wisdom, and his warriors fight as we do—himself is alone exposed. Quick, let your aim be certain, and he dies. Our rifles were levelled, rifles which, but for him, knew not how to miss—'twas all in vain, a power mightier far than we, shielded him from harm. He cannot die in battle. I am old, and soon shall be gathered to the great councilfire of my fathers, in the land of shades, but ere I go, there is a something, bids me speak, in the voice of prophecy. Listen! The Great Spirit protects that man, and guides his destinies—he will become the chief of nations, and a people yet unborn, will hail him as the founder of a mighty empire!

After the Battles of Lexington and Concord in 1775, the Second Continental Congress was convened, and John Adams of Massachusetts nominated Washington to be Commander-in-Chief of the Continental Army. Not thinking himself "equal to the command I am honored with," Washington led an underfed, underclothed, and underpaid army against great odds to a resounding victory for the infant United States.

By 1787 it became clear that the Articles of Confederation were too weak to provide Congress with the needed powers to enforce its laws. Thus a Constitutional Convention was called to order and Washington was named presiding officer. After an unusually hot summer of equally heated debate, the new constitution was signed on September 17th. Having gained a universal respect for his strong and noble leadership, Washington was the natural choice for the first President. He was elected unanimously and, though longing for the peaceful life of Mount Vernon, took office in March 1789.

Perhaps one of Washington's greatest tasks as President was to nurture the young United States and establish it as a nation in its own right. His tenacious determination to keep the country out of foreign disputes allowed for the establishment of economic stability and military strength, which would cause America to become the greatest nation on earth.

After two terms as President, a weary Washington declined a third, longing to spend his remaining years at home as a private citizen. Vice-President, John Adams was elected to fill his seat. Concerning the Inauguration ceremonies and Washington's brief valedictory, an eyewitness gave this account:

General Washington's dress was a full suit of black. His military hat had the black cockade. There stood the "Father of his Country," acknowledged by nations — the first in war, first in peace, and first in the hearts of his countrymen. No marshals with gold-colored scarfs attended him—there was no cheering—no noise; the most profound silence greeted him, as if the great assembly desired to hear him breathe, and catch his breath in homage of their hearts. Mr. Adams covered his face with both his hands; the sleeves of his coat, and his hands, were covered with tears. Every now and then there was a suppressed sob. I cannot describe Washington's appearance as I felt it— perfectly composed and self-possessed, till the close of his address; Then, when strong nervous sobs broke loose, when tears covered the faces, then the great man was shaken. I never took my eyes from his face. Large drops came from his eyes. He looked to the youthful children who were parting with their father, their friend, as if his heart was with them, and would be to the end.

For the last two years of his life, the beloved ex-president enjoyed the sweet presence of his family at Mount Vernon. He received many guests from across the country and the world. At ten o'clock on the evening of December 14, 1799, after catching a cold from riding his horse in the rain, America's immortal hero died, being "first in war, first in peace, and first in the hearts of his countrymen."

26
Noah Webster
1758-1843

One of the leading educators of his day, Noah Webster gained lasting fame for his *American Dictionary of the English Language,* the most authoritative work of its kind up to that time. It contained twelve thousand words never yet to appear in a dictionary.

Shorter than average, vain, and contentious, Webster was a nationalist of tremendous energy. His many talents included: historian, lawyer, journalist, teacher, and politician. He had an intensity that overwhelmed his opponents, coupled with a high pitched voice that irritated them as well. A descendant of Governor William Bradford of the Plymouth colony, he served as a volunteer in the Revolutionary War and afterwards, though licensed to practice law, he chose to teach school.

The education of children seemed to be his first love. And one of the chief ends of that education, he believed, was a thorough acquaintance with American history. He wrote,

As soon as (a child) opens his lips, he should rehearse the history of his own country; he should lisp the praise of liberty and of those illustrious heroes and statesmen who have wrought a revolution in her favor.

Dr. Ramsay, in his *History of the American Revolution,* wrote, "The principles of their mother tongue were first unfolded to the Americans since the Revolution by their countryman Webster. Pursuing an unbeaten track, he has made discoveries in the genius and construction of the English language which had escaped the researches of preceding philologists."

In the national debate over the Constitution, Webster lent his extraordinary talents to the Federalist cause. In 1787 he became editor of *The American Magazine,* writing many powerful articles in support of a strong national government.

He felt strongly that the American character would be molded and unified by means of individual integrity. He once exhorted American citizens to "unshackle your minds, and act like independent beings. You have an empire to raise and support by your exertions and a national character to establish and extend by your wisdom and virtue." On another occasion he wrote, "The virtues of men are of more consequence to society than their abilities, and for this reason the heart should be cultivated with more assiduity than the head."

After his death, at eighty-five years of age, Webster's heirs sold the dictionary rights to the G. and C. Merriam Company.

27
James Winthrop
1752-1821

A fifth generation descendant of John Winthrop, first governor of the Massachusetts Bay Colony, the twenty three year old James Winthrop rushed from his post as librarian at Harvard University when he heard of the fighting at nearby Bunker Hill. He was wounded in the ensuing battle on June 17, 1775, but still returned to the college where he found that all the books had been removed from the library for safe keeping.

In 1786, Daniel Shays and his followers forcibly released several prisoners and closed the courts that convicted them in what became known as Shays' Rebellion. Winthrop was part of the Massachusetts militia, which successfully quelled the uprising.

An active participant in the debates over ratification of the Federal Constitution, Winthrop was a skilled advocate of states' rights. In his powerful writings, he opposed excessive consolidation of federal power as inconsistent with republican principles. His articles were recognized by the signature "Agrippa."

The New England patriot was distinguished, not only as a soldier and an able statesman, but for his historical and scientific investigations as well. His depth of learning could not match a Madison or an Adams, but it was nevertheless broad in its range of comprehension. Biblical studies were also an object of his pursuits, having written a work entitled *An Attempt to Translate Part of the Apocalypse of St. John into Familiar Language*. Having mastered all the common languages, he took up Russian and Chinese in his old age.

James Winthrop died at the age of sixty-nine in the town of his nativity, Cambridge, Massachusetts.

28
John Witherspoon
1723-1794

When John Adams rose from his seat in the Congress of 1776, and declared that the colonies were ripe for independence, John Witherspoon, a delegate from New Jersey, scanned the room and added, "Some colonies are rotten for the want of it!" That day the Declaration of Independence was signed by Witherspoon, along with fifty-five others, as the document was unanimously adopted. And that timely comment from the Scottish immigrant, as well as his ensuing support for independence, led Adams to write, "Dr. Witherspoon enters with great spirit into the American cause. He seems as hearty a friend as any of the natives, an animated Son of Liberty."

A Presbyterian minister, Witherspoon had come to America upon the urging of Richard Stockton and Benjamin Rush, both signers of the Declaration. Having become president of the College of New Jersey (later Princeton), he acquired a wide sphere of influence. Many of his students were to become vital participants in the celebrated events of that turbulent era. James Madison was one of them. Rush wrote of the Doctor:

The College flourished under him for many years. He gave a new turn to education, and spread taste and correctness in literature throughout the United States. It was easy to distinguish his pupils everywhere whenever they spoke or wrote for the public.

The only clergyman in Congress, Witherspoon was a prolific writer as well, contributing greatly to patriotic, educational, and religious causes by means of his sermons and articles. He carried himself with a wonderful dignity, and was said to be one of the few men of his day who, in that regard, could be compared to George Washington.

After Witherspoon's death at the age of seventy-one, Rush gave one last compliment to his departed friend: "A well informed statesman and remarkably luminous and correct in all his speeches . . . He was a zealous Whig, but free from the illiberality which sometimes accompanies zeal."

PART THREE

-Documents-

THE DECLARATION OF INDEPENDENCE

IN CONGRESS, JULY 4, 1776

The UNANIMOUS DECLARATION of the thirteen united STATES OF AMERICA.

WHEN in the course of human events it becomes necessary for one people to dissolve the political bands which have connected them with another, and to assume among the powers of the earth, the separate and equal station to which the laws of nature and of nature's God entitle them, a decent respect to the opinions of mankind requires that they should declare the causes which impel them to the separation.—We hold these truths to be self-evident, that all men are created equal, that they are endowed by their Creator with certain inalienable rights, that among these are life, liberty and the pursuit of happiness. That to secure these rights, governments are instituted among men, deriving their just powers from the consent of the governed,—That whenever any form of government becomes destructive of these ends, it is the right of the people to alter or to abolish it, and to institute new government, laying its foundation on such principles and organizing its powers in such form, as to them shall seem most likely to effect their safety and happiness. Prudence, indeed, will dictate that governments long established should not be changed for light and transient causes; and accordingly all experience hath shown that mankind are more disposed to suffer, while evils are sufferable, than to right themselves by abolishing the forms to which they are accustomed. But when a long train of abuses and usurpations, pursuing invariably the same object evinces a design to reduce them under absolute despotism, it is their right, it is their duty, to throw off such government, and to provide new guards for their future security.—Such has been the patient sufferances of these colonies; and such is now the necessity which constrains them to alter their former systems of government. The history of the present king of Great Britain is a history of repeated injuries and usurpations, all having in direct object the establishment of an absolute tyranny over these states. To prove this, let facts be submitted to a candid world:

• He has refused his assent to laws, the most wholesome and necessary for the public good.

• He has forbidden his governors to pass laws of immediate and pressing importance, unless suspended in their operation till his assent should be obtained; and when so suspended, he has utterly neglected to attend to them.

• He has refused to pass other laws for the accommodation of large districts of people, unless those people would relinquish the right of representation in the legislature, a right inestimable to them and formidable to tyrants only.

• He has called together legislative bodies at places unusual, uncomfortable, and distant from the depository of their public records, for the sole purpose of fatiguing them into compliance with his measures.

• He has dissolved representative houses repeatedly, for opposing with manly firmness his invasions on the rights of the people.

• He has refused for a long time, after such dissolutions, to cause others to be elected; whereby the legislative powers, incapable of annihilation, have returned to the people at large for their exercise; the state remaining in the mean time exposed to all the dangers of invasion from without, and convulsions within.

• He has endeavoured to prevent the population of these states; for that purpose obstructing the laws for naturalization of foreigners; refusing to pass others to encourage their migrations hither, and raising the conditions of new appropriations of lands.

• He has obstructed the administration of justice, by refusing his assent to laws for establishing judiciary powers.

• He has made judges dependent on his will alone, for the tenure of their offices, and the amount and payment of their salaries.

• He has erected a multitude of new offices, and sent hither swarms of officers to harass our people, and eat out their substance. He has kept among us, in times of peace, standing armies without the consent of our legislatures.

• He has affected to render the military independent of and superior to the civil Power.

• He has combined with others to subject us to a jurisdiction foreign to our constitution, and unacknowledged by our laws; giving his assent to their acts of pretended legislation:

• For quartering large bodies of armed troops among us:

• For protecting them, by a mock trial, from punishment for any murders which they should commit on the inhabitants of these states:

• For cutting off our trade with all parts of the world:

• For imposing taxes on us without our consent:

• For depriving us in many cases, of the benefits of trial by jury:

• For transporting us beyond seas to be tried for pretended offences:

• For abolishing the free system of English laws in a neighbouring province, establishing therein an arbitrary government, and enlarging its boundaries so as to render it at once an example and fit instrument for introducing the same absolute rule into these colonies:

- For taking away our charters, abolishing our most valuable laws and altering fundamentally the forms of our governments:
- For suspending our own legislatures, and declaring themselves invested with power to legislate for us in all cases whatsoever.
- He has abdicated government here, by declaring us out of his protection and waging war against us.
- He has plundered our seas, ravaged our coasts, burnt our towns, and destroyed the lives of our people.
- He is at this time transporting large armies of foreign mercenaries to complete the works of death, desolation and tyranny, already begun with circumstances of cruelty and perfidy scarcely paralleled in the most barbarous ages, and totally unworthy the Head of a civilized nation.
- He has excited domestic insurrections amongst us, and has endeavoured to bring on the inhabitants of our frontiers, the merciless Indian savages, whose known rule of warfare, is an undistinguished destruction of all ages, sexes and conditions.

In every stage of these oppressions we have petitioned for redress in the most humble terms: Our repeated petitions have been answered only by repeated injury. A prince, whose character is thus marked by every act which may define a tyrant, is unfit to be the ruler of a free people. Nor have we been wanting in attentions to our British brethren. We have warned them from time to time of attempts by their legislature to extend an unwarranted jurisdiction over us. We have reminded them of the circumstances of our emigration and settlement here. We have appealed to their native justice and magnanimity, and we have conjured them by the ties of our common kindred to disavow these usurpations, which would inevitably interrupt our connections and correspondence. They too have been deaf to the voice of justice and of consanguinity. We must, therefore, acquiesce in the necessity, which denounces our separation, and hold them, as we hold the rest of mankind, enemies in war, in peace friends.

WE, THEREFORE, the representatives of the UNITED STATES OF AMERICA, in general congress, assembled, appealing to the Supreme Judge of the world for the rectitude of our intentions, do, in the name, and by authority of the good people of these colonies, solemnly publish and declare, that these United Colonies are, and of right ought to be FREE AND INDEPENDENT STATES; that they are absolved from all allegiance to the British Crown, and that all political connection between them and the State of Great Britain, is and ought to be totally dissolved; and that as free and independent states, they have full power to levy war, conclude peace, contract alliances, establish commerce, and to do all other acts and things which independent states may of right do.—And for the support of this Declaration, with a firm reliance on the protection of Divine Providence, we mutually pledge to each other our lives, our fortunes and our sacred honor.

John Hancock	Benj. Harrison	Lewis Morris
Button Gwinnett	Thos. Nelson Jr.	Richd. Stockton
Lyman Hall	Francis Lightfoot Lee	J. Witherspoon
Geo. Walton	Carter Braxton	Fras. Hopkinson
Wm. Hooper	Robt. Morris	John Hart
Joseph Hewes	Benjamin Rush	Abra. Clark
John Penn	Benj. Franklin	Josiah Bartlett
Edward Rutledge	John Morton	Wm. Whipple
Thos. Heyward, Jr.	Geo. Clymer	Saml. Adams
Thomas Lynch, Jr.	Jas. Smith	Robt. Treat Paine
Arthur Middleton	Geo. Taylor	Elbridge Gerry
Samuel Chase	James Wilson	Step. Hopkins
Wm. Paca	Geo. Ross	John Adams
William Ellery	Caesar Rodney	Roger Sherman
Charles Carrol	Tho. McKean	Sam. Huntington
George Wythe	Wm. Floyd	Wm. Williams
Richard Henry Lee	Phil. Livingston	Oliver Wolcott
Th. Jefferson	Frans. Lewis	Matthew Thornton
Thos. Stone		

THE CONSTITUTION OF THE UNITED STATES

We the people of the United States, in order to form a more perfect Union, establish justice, insure domestic tranquility, provide for the common defense, promote the general welfare, and secure the blessings of liberty to ourselves and our posterity, do ordain and establish this Constitution for the United States of America.

ARTICLE I

Section 1. All legislative powers herein granted shall be vested in a Congress of the United States, which shall consist of a Senate and House of Representatives.

Section 2. The House of Representatives shall be composed of members chosen every second year by the people of the several states, and the electors in each state shall have the qualifications requisite for electors of the most numerous branch of the state legislature.

No person shall be a representative who shall not have attained to the age of twenty five years, and been seven years a citizen of the United States, and who shall not, when elected, be an inhabitant of that state in which he shall be chosen.

Representatives and direct taxes shall be apportioned among the several states which may be included within this Union, according to their respective numbers, which shall be determined by adding to the whole number of free persons, including those bound to service for a term of years, and excluding Indians not taxed, three-fifths of all other persons. The actual enumeration shall be made within three years after the first meeting of the Congress of the United States, and within every subsequent term of ten years, in such manner as they shall be law direct. The number of representatives shall not exceed one for every thirty thousand, but each state shall have at least one representative; and until such enumeration shall be made, the state of New Hampshire shall be entitled to choose three, Massachusetts eight, Rhode island and Providence Plantations one, Connecticut five, New York six, New Jersey four, Pennsylvania eight, Delaware one, Maryland six, Virginia ten, North Carolina five, South Carolina five, and Georgia three.

When vacancies happen in the representation from any state, the executive authority thereof shall issue writs of election to fill such vacancies.

The House of Representatives shall choose their speaker and other officers and shall have the sole power of impeachment.

Section 3. The Senate of the United States shall be composed of two senators from each state, chosen by the legislature thereof, for six years; and each senator shall have one vote.

Immediately after they shall be assembled in consequence of the first election, they shall be divided as equally as may be into three classes. The seats of the senators of the first class shall be vacated at the expiration of the second year, of the second class at the expiration of the fourth year, and of the third class at the expiration of the sixth year, so that one third may be chosen every second year; and if vacancies happen by resignation, or otherwise, during the recess of the legislature of any state, the executive thereof may make temporary appointments until the next meeting of the legislature, which shall then fill such vacancies.

No person shall be a senator who shall not have attained to the age of thirty years, and been nine years a citizen of the United States, and who shall not, when elected, be an inhabitant of that state for which he shall be chosen.

The vice-president of the United States shall be president of the Senate, but shall have no vote, unless they be equally divided.

The Senate shall choose their other officers, and also a president pre tempore, in the absence of the vice-president, or when he shall exercise the office of President of the United States.

The Senate shall have the sole power to try all impeachments. When sitting for that purpose, they shall be on oath or affirmation. When the President of the United States is tried, the chief justice shall preside; And no person shall be convicted without the concurrence of two-thirds of the members present.

Judgment in cases of impeachment shall not extend further than to removal from office, and disqualification to hold and enjoy any office of honor, trust or profit under the United States; but the party convicted shall nevertheless be liable and subject to indictment, trial, judgment and punishment, according to law.

Section 4. The times, places and manner of holding elections for senators and representatives, shall be prescribed in each state by the legislature thereof; but the Congress may at any time by law make or alter such regulations, except as to the places of choosing senators.

The Congress shall assemble at least once in every year, and such meeting shall be on the first Monday in December, unless they shall by law appoint a different day.

Section 5. Each house shall be the judge of the elections, returns, and qualifications of its own members, and a majority of each shall constitute a quorum to do business; but a smaller number may adjourn from day to day, and may be authorized to compel the attendance of absent members, in such manner and under such penalties as each house may provide.

Each house may determine the rules of its proceedings, punish its members for disorderly behavior, and, with the concurrence of two-thirds, expel a member.

Each house shall keep a journal if its proceedings and from time to time publish the same, excepting such parts as may in their judgment require secrecy; and the yeas and nays of the members of either house on any question shall, at the desire of one-fifth of those present, be entered on the journal.

Neither house, during the session of Congress, shall, without the consent of the other, adjourn for more than three days, nor to any other place than that in which the two houses shall be sitting.

Section 6. The senators and representatives shall receive a compensation for their services, to be ascertained by law, and paid out of the Treasury of the United States. They shall in all cases, except treason, felony, and breach of the peace, be privileged from arrest during their attendance at the session of their respective houses, and in going to and returning from the same; and for any speech or debate in either house, they shall not be questioned in any other place.

No senator or representative shall, during the time for which he was elected, be appointed to any civil office under the authority of the United States which shall have been created, or the emoluments whereof shall have been increased, during such time; and no person holding any office under the United States shall be a member of either house during his continuance in office.

Section 7. All bills for raising revenue shall originate in the House of Representatives; but the Senate may propose or concur with amendments as on other bills.

Every bill which shall have passed the House of Representatives and the Senate shall, before it become a law, be presented to the President of the United States. If he approve he shall sign it, but if not, he shall return it, with his objections, to that house in which it shall have originated, who shall enter the objections at large on their journal and proceed to reconsider it. If, after such reconsideration, two-thirds of that house shall agree to pass the bill, it shall be sent, together with the objections, to the other house, by which it shall likewise be reconsidered, and, if approved by two-thirds of that house, it shall become a law. But in all such cases the votes of both houses shall be determined by yeas and nays, and the names of the persons voting for and against the bills shall be entered on the journal of each house respectively. If any bill shall not be returned by the President within ten days (Sundays excepted) after it shall have been presented to him, the same shall be a law, in like manner as if he had signed it, unless the Congress by their adjournment prevent its return, in which case it shall not be a law.

Every order, resolution, or vote to which the concurrence of the Senate and House of Representatives may be necessary (except on a question of adjournment) shall be presented to the President of the United States; and before the same shall take effect, shall be approved by him, or being disapproved by him, shall be repassed by two-thirds of the Senate and House of Representatives, according to the rules and limitations prescribed in the case of a bill.

Section 8. The Congress shall have power to lay and collect taxes, duties, imposts, and excises, to pay the debts and provide for the common defense and general welfare of the United States; but all duties, imposts, and excises shall be uniform throughout the United States;

To borrow money on the credit of the United States;

To regulate commerce with foreign nations, and among the several states, and with the Indian tribes;

To establish a uniform rule of naturalization and uniform laws on the subject of bankruptcies throughout the United States;

To coin money, regulate the value thereof, and of foreign coin, and fix the standard of weights and measures;

To provide for the punishment of counterfeiting the securities and current coin of the United States;

To establish post offices and post roads;

To promote the progress of science and useful arts, by securing for limited times to authors and inventors the exclusive right to their respective writings and discoveries;

To constitute tribunals inferior to the Supreme Court;

To define and punish piracies and felonies committed on the high seas and offenses against the law of nations;

To declare war, grant letters of marque and reprisal, and make rules concerning captures on land and water;

To raise and support armies, but no appropriation of money to that use shall be for a longer term than two years;

To provide and maintain a navy;

To make rules for the government and regulation of the land and naval forces;

To provide for calling forth the militia to execute the laws of the Union, suppress insurrections, and repel invasions;

To provide for organizing, arming, and disciplining the militia, and for governing such part of them as may be employed in the service of the United States, reserving to the states respectively the appointment of the officers and the authority of training the militia according to the discipline prescribed by Congress;

To exercise exclusive legislation in all cases whatsoever over such district (not exceeding ten miles square) as may, by cession of particular states and the acceptance of Congress, become the seat of the government of the United States, and to exercise like authority over all places purchased by the consent of the legislature of the state in which the same shall be for the erection of forts, magazines, arsenals, dockyards, and other needful buildings; and

To make all laws which shall be necessary and proper for carrying into execution the foregoing powers and all other powers vested by this Constitution in the government of the United States, or in any department or officer thereof.

Section 9. The migration or importation of such persons as any of the states now existing shall think proper to admit shall not be prohibited by the Congress prior to the year 1808, but a tax or duty may be imposed on such importation, not exceeding ten dollars for each person.

The privilege of the writ of habeas corpus shall not be suspended, unless, when in cases of rebellion or invasion, the public safety may require it.

No bill of attainder or ex post facto law shall be passed.

No capitation or other direct tax shall be laid, unless in proportion to the census or enumeration hereinbefore directed to be taken.

No tax or duty shall be laid on articles exported from any state.

No preference shall be given by any regulation of commerce or revenue to the ports of one state over those of another; nor shall vessels bound to or from one state be obliged to enter, clear, or pay duties in another.

No money shall be drawn from the Treasury but in consequence of appropriations made by law; and a regular statement and account of the receipts and expenditures of all public money shall be published from time to time.

No title of nobility shall be granted by the United States. And no person holding any office of profit or trust under them shall, without the consent of the Congress, accept of any kind whatever from any king, prince, or foreign state.

Section 10. No state shall enter into any treaty, alliance, or confederation; grant letters of marque and reprisal; coin money; emit bills of credit; make anything but gold and silver coin a tender in payment of debts; pass any bill of attainder, ex post facto law, or law impairing the obligation of contracts, or grant any title of nobility.

No state shall, without the consent of the Congress, lay any imposts or duties on imports or exports, except what may be absolutely necessary for executing its inspection laws; and the net produce of all duties and imposts laid by any state on imports or exports shall be for the use of the Treasury of the United States; and all such laws shall be subject to the revision and control of the Congress.

No state shall, without the consent of Congress, lay any duty of tonnage; keep troops or ships of war in time of peace; enter into any agreement or compact with another state or with a foreign power, or engage in war, unless actually invaded, or in such imminent danger as will not admit of delay.

ARTICLE II

Section 1. The executive power shall be vested in a President of the United States of America. He shall hold his office during the term of four years, and, together with the vice-president, chosen for the same term,- be elected as follows;

Each state shall appoint, in such manner as the legislature thereof may direct, a number of electors, equal to the whole number of senators and representatives to which the state may be entitled in the Congress; but no senator or representative, or person holding an office of trust or profit under the United States, shall be appointed an elector.

The electors shall meet in their respective states and vote by ballot for two persons, of whom one at least shall not be an inhabitant of the same state with themselves. And they shall make a list of all the persons voted for and of the number of votes for each; which list they shall sign and certify, and transmit sealed to the seat of the government of the United States, directed to the president of the Senate. The president of the Senate shall, in the presence of the Senate and House of Representatives, open all the certificates, and the votes shall then be counted. The person having the greatest number of votes shall be the President, if such number be a majority of the whole number of electors appointed; and if there be more than one who have such majority, and have an equal number of votes, then the House of Representatives shall immediately choose by ballot one of them for President; and if no person have a majority, then from the five highest on the list the said house shall in like manner choose the President. But in choosing the President, the votes shall be taken by states, the representation from each state having one vote; a quorum for this purpose shall consist of a member or members from two-thirds of the states, and a majority of all the states shall be necessary to a choice. In every case, after the choice of the President, the person having the greatest number of votes of the electors shall be the vice-president. But if there should remain two or more who have equal votes, the Senate shall choose from them by ballot the vice-president.

The Congress may determine the time of choosing the electors and the day on which they shall give their votes, which day shall be the same throughout the United States.

No person except a natural-born citizen, or a citizen of the United States at the time of the adoption of this Constitution, shall be eligible to the office of President; neither shall any person be eligible to that office who shall not have attained to the age of thirty-five years and been fourteen years a resident within the United States.

In case of the removal of the President from office, or of his death, resignation, or inability to discharge the powers and duties of the said office, the same shall devolve on the vice-president, and the Congress may by law provide for the case of removal, death, resignation, or inability, both of the President and vice-president, declaring what officer shall then act as President; and such officer shall act accordingly until the disability be removed or a President shall be elected.

The President shall, at stated times, receive for his services a compensation, which shall neither be increased nor diminished during the period for which he shall have been elected; and he shall not receive within that period any other emolument from the United States or any of them.

Before he enter on the execution of his office, he shall take the following oath or affirmation: "I do solemnly swear (or affirm) that I will faithfully execute the office of President of the United States, and will, to the best of my ability, preserve, protect and defend the Constitution of the United States."

Section 2. The President shall be commander in chief of the Army and Navy of the United States, and of the militia of the several states when called into the actual service of the United States. He may require the opinion, in writing, of the principal officer in each of the executive departments upon any subject relating to the duties of their respective offices. And he shall have power to grant reprieves and pardons for offenses against the United States, except in cases of impeachment.

He shall have power, by and with the advice and consent of the Senate, to make treaties, provided two-thirds of the senators present concur; and he shall nominate, and by and with the advice and consent of the Senate, shall appoint ambassadors, other public ministers and consuls, judges of the Supreme Court, and all other officers of the United States whose appointments are not herein otherwise provided for, and which shall be established by law; but the Congress may by law vest the appointment of such inferior officers as they think proper in the President alone, in the courts of law, or in the heads of departments.

The President shall have power to fill up all vacancies that may happen during the recess of the Senate, by granting commissions which shall expire at the end of their next session.

Section 3. He shall from time to time give to the Congress information of the state of the Union, and recommend to their consideration such measures as he shall judge necessary and expedient; he may, on extraordinary occasions, convene both houses, or either of them, and in case of disagreement between them with respect to the time of adjournment, he may adjourn them to such time as he shall think proper; he shall receive ambassadors and other public ministers; he shall take care that the laws be faithfully executed; and shall commission all the officers of the United States.

Section 4. The President, vice-president, and all civil officers of the United States shall be removed from office on impeachment for, and conviction of, treason, bribery, or other high crimes and misdemeanors.

ARTICLE III

Section 1. The judicial power of the United States shall be vested in one Supreme Court, and in such inferior courts as the Congress may from time to time ordain and establish. The judges, both of the Supreme and inferior courts, shall hold their offices during good behavior, and shall, at stated times, receive for their services a compensation which shall not be diminished during their continuance in office.

Section 2. The judicial power shall extend to all cases, in law and equity, arising under this Constitution, the laws of the United States, and treaties made, or which shall be made, under their authority; to all cases affecting ambassadors, other public ministers and consuls; to all cases of Admiralty and maritime jurisdiction; to controversies to which the United States shall be a party; to controversies between two or more states; between a state and citizens of another state; between citizens of different states; between citizens of the same state claiming lands under grants of different states; and between a state, or the citizens thereof, and foreign states, citizens, or subjects.

In all cases affecting ambassadors, other public ministers, and consuls, and those in which a state shall be a party, the Supreme Court shall have original jurisdiction. In all the other cases beforementioned, the Supreme Court shall have appellate jurisdiction, both as to law and fact, with such exceptions and under such regulations as the Congress shall make.

The trial of all crimes, except in cases of impeachment, shall be by jury; and such trial shall be held in the state where the said crimes shall have been committed; but when not committed within any state, the trial shall be at such place or places as the Congress may by law have directed.

Section 3. Treason against the United States shall consist only in levying war against them, or in adhering to their enemies, giving them aid and comfort. No person shall be convicted of treason unless on the testimony of two witnesses to the same overt act, or on confession in open court.

The Congress shall have power to declare the punishment of treason, but no attainder of treason shall work corruption of blood or forfeiture except during the life of the person attainted.

ARTICLE IV

Section 1. Full faith and credit shall be given in each state to the public acts, records, and judicial proceedings of every other state. And the Congress may by general laws prescribe the manner in which such acts, records, and proceedings shall be proved, and the effect thereof.

Section 2. The citizens of each state shall be entitled to all privileges and immunities of citizens in the several states.

A person charged in any state with treason, felony, or other crime, who shall flee from justice and be found in another state, shall, on demand of the executive authority of the state from which he fled, be delivered up to be removed to the state having jurisdiction of the crime.

No person held to service or labor in one state under the laws thereof, escaping into another, shall, in consequence of any law or regulation therein, be discharged from such service or labor, but shall be delivered up on claim of the party to whom such service or labor may be due.

Section 3. New states may be admitted by the Congress into this Union; but no new state shall be formed or erected within the jurisdiction of any other state; nor any state be formed by the junction of two or more states, or parts of states, without the consent of the legislatures of the states concerned as well as of the Congress.

The Congress shall have power to dispose of and make all needful rules and regulations respecting the territory or other property belonging to the United States; and nothing in this Constitution shall be so construed as to prejudice any claims of the United States, or of any particular state.

Section 4. The United States shall guarantee to every state in this Union a republican form of government, and shall protect each of them against invasion, and, on application of the legislature or of the executive (when the legislature cannot be convened), against domestic violence.

ARTICLE V

The Congress, whenever two-thirds of both houses shall deem it necessary, shall propose amendments to this Constitution or, on the application of the legislatures of two-thirds of the several states, shall call a convention for proposing amendments, which, in either case, shall be valid, to all intents and purposes, as part of this Constitution when ratified by the legislatures of three-fourths of the several states, or by conventions in three-fourths thereof, as the one or the other mode of ratification may be proposed by the Congress; provided that no amendment which may be made prior to the year 1808 shall in any manner affect the first and fourth clauses in the 9th Section of the 1st Article; and that no state, without its consent, shall be deprived of its equal suffrage in the Senate.

ARTICLE VI

All debts contracted and engagements entered into before the adoption of this Constitution shall be as valid against the United States under this Constitution as under the Confederation.

This Constitution and the laws of the United States which shall be made in pursuance thereof, and all treaties made, or which shall be made, under the authority of the United States, shall be the supreme law of the land; and the judges in every state shall be bound thereby, anything in the constitution or laws of any state to the contrary notwithstanding.

The senators and representatives beforementioned, and the members of the several state legislatures, and all executive and judicial officers, both of the United States and of the several states, shall be bound by oath or affirmation to support this Constitution; but no religious test shall ever be required as a qualification to any office or public trust under the United States.

ARTICLE VII

The ratification of the conventions of nine states shall be sufficient for the establishment of this constitution between the states so ratifying the same.

DONE in convention, by the unanimous consent of the states present, the seventeenth day of September, in the year of our Lord one thousand seven hundred and eighty-seven, and of the independence of the United States of America the twelfth. In witness whereof, we have hereunto subscribed our names.

GEORGE WASHINGTON,
President, and Deputy from Virginia.

NEW-HAMPSHIRE   John Langdon
                         Nicholas Gilman

MASSACHUSETTS   Nathaniel Gorham
                         Rufus King

CONNECTICUT   William Samuel Johnson
                         Roger Sherman

NEW YORK	Alexander Hamilton
NEW JERSEY	William Livingston
	David Brearley
	William Paterson
	Jonathan Dayton
PENNSYLVANIA	Benjamin Franklin
	Thomas Mifflin
	Robert Morris
	George Clymer
	Thomas Fitzsimons
	Jared Ingersoll
	James Wilson
	Gouverneur Morris
DELAWARE	George Read
	Gunning Bedford, Jr.
	John Dickinson
	Richard Bassett
	Jacob Broom
MARYLAND	James McHenry
	Daniel Jenifer of St. Thos.
	Daniel Carroll
VIRGINIA	John Blair
	James Madison, Jr.
NORTH CAROLINA	William Blount
	Richard D. Spaight
	Hugh Williamson
SOUTH CAROLINA	John Rutledge
	Charles C. Pinckney
	Charles Pinckney
	Pierce Butler
GEORGIA	William Few
	Abraham Baldwin
Attest.	WILLIAM JACKSON, secretary

THE
BILL OF RIGHTS

ARTICLE I

Congress shall make no law respecting an establishment of religion or prohibiting the free exercise thereof, or abridging the freedom of speech or of the press, or the right of the people peaceably to assemble and to petition the government for a redress of grievances.

ARTICLE II

A well regulated militia being necessary to the security of a free state, the right of the people to keep and bear arms shall not be infringed.

ARTICLE III

No soldier shall, in time of peace, be quartered in any house without the consent of the owner, nor in time of war but in a manner to be prescribed by law.

ARTICLE IV

The right of the people to be secure in their persons, houses, papers, and effects against unreasonable searches and seizures shall not be violated, and no warrants shall issue, but upon probable cause, supported by oath or affirmation, and particularly describing the place to be searched and the persons or things to be seized.

ARTICLE V

No person shall be held to answer for a capital or otherwise infamous crime unless on a presentment or indictment of a grand jury, except in cases arising in the land or naval forces, or in the militia, when in actual service in time of war or public danger; nor shall any person be subject for the same offense to be twice put in jeopardy of life or limb; nor shall be compelled in any criminal case to be a witness against himself, nor be deprived of life, liberty, or property without due process of law; nor shall private property be taken for public use without just compensation.

ARTICLE VI

In all criminal prosecutions, the accused shall enjoy the right to a speedy and public trial by an impartial jury of the state and district wherein the crime shall have been committed, which district shall have been previously ascertained by law, and to be informed of the nature and cause of the accusation; to be confronted with the witnesses against him; to have compulsory process for obtaining witnesses in his favor, and to have the assistance of counsel for his defense.

ARTICLE VII

In suits at common law, where the value in controversy shall exceed twenty dollars, the right of trial by jury shall be preserved, and no fact tried by a jury shall be otherwise reexamined in any court of the United States than according to the rules of the common law.

ARTICLE VIII

Excessive bail shall not be required, nor excessive fines imposed, nor cruel and unusual punishments inflicted.

ARTICLE IX

The enumeration in the Constitution of certain rights shall not be construed to deny or disparage others retained by the people.

ARTICLE X

The powers not delegated to the United States by the Constitution, nor prohibited by it to the states, are reserved to the states respectively, or to the people.

Bibliography

Adams, Charles Francis, *The Works of John Adams, 10 vols.*, Boston, 1851

Alden, John R., *A History of the American Revolution*, New York: Alfred A. Knopf, 1969

Allan, Herbert S., *John Hancock: Patriot in Purple*, New York: The Macmillan Co., 1948

Bailyn, Bernard (Ed.), *Debate on the Constitution, 2 vols.*, New York: The Library of America, 1993

Benjamin Franklin: Writings, New York: Library Classics of the U.S., Inc., 1987

Binger, Carl, *Revolutionary Doctor: Benjamin Rush*, New York: W.W. Norton & Co., 1966

Butterfield, L.H., *Diary and Autobiography of John Adams 4 vols.*, Cambridge: Belknap Press of Harvard University Press, 1961

Carson, Hampton L. (Ed.), *One Hundredth Anniversary of the Framing of the Constitution of the United States, 2 vols.*, Philadelphia: J.B. Lippencott Co., 1889

Commager, Henry Steele (Ed.), *Documents of American History*, New York: Appleton-Century-Crofts, Division of Commager, Henry Steele and Morris, Richard B., The Spirit of 76, New York: Harper and Row, 1958

Corner, George W. (Ed.), *The Autobiography of Benjamin Rush*, New Jersey: Princeton University Press, 1948

Custis, George Washington, *Private Memoirs of Washington*, Edgewood Publishing Company, 1859

DeNovo, John A. (Ed.), *Selected Readings in American History,* New York: Charles Scribner's Sons, 1969

Dorson, Richard M. (Ed.), *America Rebels,* New York: Pantheon Books, 1953

Encyclopedia Britannica, *The Annals of America, 4 vols.,* Chicago, *1968*

Fitzpatrick, John C. (Ed.), *The Writings of George Washington, 37 vols.,* Washington D.C.: U.S. Gov. Printing Office, 1940

Fleming, Thomas, *1776: Year of Illusions,* New York: W.W. Norton & Co., 1975

Flexner, James Thomas, *The Young Hamilton,* Boston & Toronto: Little, Brown and Company, 1978

Forbes, Esther, *Paul Revere & The World He Lived In,* Boston: Houghton Mifflin Co., 1942

Ford, Paul Leicester (Ed.), *Pamphlets on the Constitution of the United States,* New York: Da Capo Press, 1968

Ford, Paul Leicester (Ed.), *The Writings of John Dickinson, 3 vols.,* Philadelphia: The Historical Society of PA. 1895

Frisch, Morton J. (Ed.), *Selected Writings and Speeches of Alexander Hamilton,* Washington and London: American Enterprise for Public Policy Research, 1985

Harnsburger, Caroline Thomas, *Treasury of Presidential Quotes,* Chicago: Follett Publishing Company, 1964

Hosmer, James K., Morse, John T. (Ed.), *Samuel Adams,* Boston & New York: Houghton, Mifflin & Co., 1885

Hutchinson, Wil. T. and Wil. M.E. Rachal, Wil. M.E. (Eds.), *The Papers of James Madison, 17 vols.,* Chicago: Univ. of Chicago Press, 1962

Jensen, Merrill (Ed.), *Tracts of the American Revolution,* Indianapolis: Bobbs-Merrill Company, Inc., 1967

Kane, Joseph Nathan, *Facts about the Presidents,* New York: The H.W. Wilson Co., 1981

Kriegel, Leonard (Ed.), *Essential Works of the Founding Fathers,* New York: Bantam books, 1964

LaPierre, Wayne, *Guns, Crime, and Freedom,* Washington D.C.: Regnery Publ. Co., 1994

Lewis, John D. (Ed.), *Anti-Federalists Versus Federalists: Selected Documents,* Scranton, PA: Chandler Publ. Co., 1967

Main, Jackson Turner, *The Antifederalists: Critics of the Constitution,* Chapel Hill: University of N.C. Press, 1961

Malone, Dumas (Ed.), *Dictionary of American Biography, vols. 17 & 20,* New York: Charles Scribner's Sons, 1936

Malone, Dumas (Text), *The Story of the Declaration of Independence,* New York: Oxford University Press, 1954

Marshall, Peter and Manuel, David, *The Light and the Glory,* New Jersey: Fleming H. Revell Co., 1977

Marx, Karl and Engels, Freidrich, *The Communist Manifesto,* New York: Washington Square Press, 1965

Miller, Helen Hill, *George Mason: Gentleman Revolutionary,* Chapel Hill: University of North Carolina Press, 1975

Morgan, George, *Patrick Henry,* Philadelphia and London: J.B. Lippencott Company, 1929

National Cyclopedia of American Biography, vol. 7, New York: James T. White & Co., 1897

Padover, Saul K. (Ed.), *The Complete Madison: His Basic Writings*, New York: Harper & Brothers, 1971

Padover, Saul K. (Ed.), *The Mind of Alexander Hamilton*, New York: Harper and Bros., 1958

Padover, Saul K. (Ed.), *The Washington Papers*, New York: Grosset and Dunlap, 1955

Pellew, George, T., Morse, John T. (Ed.), *John Jay*, Boston & New York: Houghton, Mifflin & Co., 1890

Rutland, Robert A. (Ed.), *The Papers of George Mason, 3 vols.*, Chapel Hill: University of North Carolina Press, 1970

Showman, Richard K. (Ed.), *The Papers of General Nathaniel Greene, 5 vols.*, Chapel Hill: University of North Carolina Press, 1976

Thayer, Theodore, *Nathaniel Greene: Strategist of the American Revolution*, New York: Twayne Publ., 1960

Thomas Jefferson: Writings, New York: Library Classics of the U.S., Inc., 1984

Thomas Paine: Collected Writings, New York: Library of America, 1995

Van Doren, Carl, *Benjamin Franklin*, New York: The Viking Press, 1938

Vaughan, Alden T. (Ed.), *Chronicles of the American Revolution*, New York: Grosset & Dunlap, 1965

Whitney, David C., *The Colonial Spirit of '76*, Illinois: J.G. Ferguson Publ. Co., 1974

Woodward, W.E., *Tom Paine: America's Godfather*, New York: E.P. Dutton & Co., 1945

Zahniser, Marvin R., *Charles Cotesworth Pinckney: Founding Father*, Chapel Hill: University of N.C. Press, 1967

Index

Order These Huntington House/VIP Books !